CANE CREEK

Cane Creek Meetinghouse, 1995

CANE CREEK
MOTHER OF MEETINGS

BY

BOBBIE T. TEAGUE

Cane Creek Monthly Meeting of Friends
North Carolina Friends Historical Society
North Carolina Yearly Meeting of Friends
1995

LIBRARY OF CONGRESS CATALOG CARD NUMBER 95–068074
ISBN NUMBER 0–942–72725–8

CANE CREEK MONTHLY MEETING OF FRIENDS
605 W. GREENSBORO–CHAPEL HILL RD., SNOW CAMP, NC 27349

NORTH CAROLINA FRIENDS HISTORICAL SOCIETY
P.O. BOX 8502, GREENSBORO, NC 27419

NORTH CAROLINA YEARLY MEETING OF FRIENDS
5506 FRIENDLY AVE., GREENSBORO, NC 27410

COMPOSED BY FRIENDLY DESKTOP PUBLISHING
PRINTED BY THOMSON–SHORE

CONTENTS

Wilma Griffin

To Wilma Griffin

I consider it a privilege and an honor to dedicate this book, *Cane Creek, Mother of Meetings*, to Wilma Griffin. It is my small way of saying "Thank you" for the support and help that she has given me during the writing of this book.

PREFACE

Cane Creek Friends Meetinghouse stands just north of the intersection of the Sylvan School Road and the Greensboro–Chapel Hill Highway in southern Alamance County, North Carolina. It is a place where people gather to worship as they have for more than 240 years. Young and old alike can find within its walls kindness, love, devotion, and inspiration. This has always been so.

It is not much different now than it was when I was a child, growing up in the Cane Creek Meeting. My memories from that time and place to the present form a kaleidoscope of pictures that seem to change, yet forever remain the same.

One of the stories that anyone who grew up in or around Cane Creek Meeting heard over and over again was the story about the time when General Cornwallis brought his British soldiers to Simon Dixon's Mill during the Revolution. As a youngster I loved stories, but to be perfectly honest, I grew rather tired of hearing that story over and over. It seemed to me that surely there should be a lot of different kinds of stories — not just one.

I found in Wilma Griffin someone who knew many stories about Cane Creek. In fact, she knows more about the history of Cane Creek and the Snow Camp area than anyone I know. She has been the historian–in–residence for Cane Creek Meeting for well over fifty years. Many people come to the area searching for their roots. Not many of them go away without learning something about their ancestors, for invariably someone will refer them to Wilma. And if Wilma doesn't know anything to tell them, their ancestors probably were not from this area!

One of the things that Wilma has worked toward and dreamed about for a long time is the publication of a history of Cane Creek

Meeting. This has been done with many of the older meetings in North Carolina Yearly Meeting, and she wanted very much to have a comparable history for Cane Creek. She made an outline for such a project and wrote a synopsis. When she learned that I had similar interests, we decided to pool our resources. She kindly placed in my hands her writing, her research, and some of her pictures. My own research included a thorough reading of the Cane Creek Minutes from the very beginning up to the present time. I also had the opportunity to do research in the Friends Historical Collection at Guilford College. I consider it a rare privilege to have put the stories, the experiences, and the facts together in what I believe is a readable and enjoyable way.

The writing of this book has given me a greater understanding of and admiration for early Friends. There is indeed more to tell about Cane Creek than just the fact that once, long ago, an English lord brought his soldiers to a grist mill located on Cane Creek. I hope that those who read this account will enjoy it and learn from it just as I have done.

I want to express my many, many thanks to the following: Mary Edith Hinshaw, David Teague, and Mary Butt for their patience and kindness during the editing process; Mike Arnold for lending his computer expertise; John C. Allen for sharing information from his research; and especially to my husband, Dwight, for his help, his support, and encouragement.

Bobbie T. Teague
Snow Camp, NC
1995

The Beginnings

Before anything there was the land. There has always been the land, a gently rolling plateau with meandering streams that find their way to the faster–moving waters of Cane Creek and on to the swiftly–flowing Haw River; a land of rich and fertile soil; a land of tall trees: hickory, poplar, and oak; a land of fragrant cedars and lofty pines; a land that was for centuries home to the red man and his *yanasa,* his buffalo; a land that Dr. John Lederer, a German, explored in 1670. He recorded a visit to Native Americans who lived on rich "soyl" (Whitaker 1). These were the Sissipahaw, one–time inhabitants of the land that today is southern Alamance County in central North Carolina.

In 1700, John Lawson, surveyor for the province of North Carolina, organized an expedition to explore the land. He described it as a beautiful wild paradise with rich soil, good timber, and plentiful game. He seemed especially fascinated with the wild "turkeyes." On the third day he reached the "Hau." He also recorded his hopes of filling the land with thousands of families. Lawson visited several of the local tribes but found only about 1,000 living in the area (Whitaker 2). By the year 1711, Indian wars had forced those to move east and join other tribes.

Hunters from Pennsylvania were also among the first white men to come to the area. It is said that one hunting party experienced such a heavy snow that they named their encampment "Snow Camp," and the name stuck. The traditionally accepted location of their camp was about one–fourth mile east of the site on which the meetinghouse would be built. While they were in the area, the hunters saw much game, streams filled with fish, fertile land, and great forests. This abundance was an inducement for them to return permanently.

The settlement of this wilderness area began as soon as peace seemed assured at the close of the Indian wars. At first a few "squatters" appeared on the scene, cleared small patches of land, and built simple one–room log cabins or three–sided shelters. When the Carolina Proprietors saw the advantage of land development, they began to offer land at bargain prices. The Granville Estates offered 640 acres for three shillings and a small quitrent, while retaining the mineral rights to the property. North Carolina governors offered fifty acres free to homesteaders. One Carolina resident wrote that 640 acres would cost no more than three or four pounds sterling and would be free from taxes (Stuart 1). Motivated by the prospect of owning large amounts of land for a small investment, many immigrants headed for the Haw River and its tributaries. To the north of the Haw came the Scotch–Irish

Presbyterians; along the western tributary, Alamance Creek, were the Lutheran and Reformed settlements; and along the southern tributary, Cane Creek, the Quakers settled.

Quakers came to the Carolinas several decades before they arrived in the backwoods country of the Piedmont. Early Friends emigrated from Scotland, England, and Ireland to the New World. They came in search of a better life. To them a better life would have included cheap acreage, freedom to pursue a livelihood of their choice, and the freedom to worship without restrictions imposed by government.

The patterns of immigration were formed and made necessary by the patterns and forms of the land itself. The great bays and harbors in the northern part of the continent beckoned the ships and their captains with promises of safe landing sites and rich soil inland. Thus, the first Quaker immigrants settled in the Tidewater and Eastern Shore of the New World.

Land along the shore farther south was not as hospitable. Great Barrier Islands blocked the entrances to the sounds and rivers. Even good sailors dreaded the shoals and treacherous coastline of the Carolinas. Therefore, the settlement of this land came not with an influx of immigrants from Europe but rather from the eastern shore of Delaware, Maryland, and New Jersey.

The first Friends to settle in the area that is now North Carolina came to the Albemarle region, to Perquimans and Pasquotank Counties, by about 1665. Their first recorded meetings for worship were held in 1672, at the present town of Hertford, when first William Edmondson, and then George Fox, visited the colony. Several meetings were set up in the coastal area, and a quarterly meeting was begun in 1681 (*Faith and Practice* 5).

In 1732, a company made up mostly of Quakers from Pennsylvania and Maryland acquired 100,000 acres of land in Frederick

County, Virginia, from the colonial government. Here, Hopewell Friends Meeting was established in 1735 (Forbish 33). This proved to be an important beachhead for the Quaker migration into piedmont North Carolina. Many of these families joined others who were moving south from Virginia, Pennsylvania, and points north into central North Carolina.

The decision to come south, to uproot their families, and to travel some 400 miles into the wilderness was not easy for the early pioneers, but many Quakers came. The first of the settlers from Pennsylvania and Maryland must have made the journey by horseback and on foot and transported supplies on pack animals. Mothers with small children rode horseback while the men often walked. Traveling was fairly easy through Virginia; however, the way grew more difficult the farther south they came. After they left the traveled route, they would most likely have followed the Great Trading Path that led to Hillsborough. They would have crossed the Haw River near the present–day village of Swepsonville, taken the lower branch of the trail at this point, and followed it into the area along Cane Creek.

A family's journey to Carolina was not undertaken without careful preparations. The first pioneers could not have used wagons on Indian footpaths; routes were widened for wagons soon after the earliest settlers came. A large wagon was needed to hold the necessary items for the journey and to establish a new home. There was no room for luxuries; everything must have a useful purpose. Occasionally some prized possession would be left in the care of a relative with the understanding that it would be brought to Carolina at a later time.

On weekdays the Friends tried to travel at least ten miles, but on the Sabbath day they rested. One can imagine the little Quaker family — or families — sitting quietly, worshiping in the dense forest. After about two months on the road, they would reach their new home, and a new life would begin at Cane Creek.

The early settlers claimed land along the stream called Cane Creek, named for the prolific amount of reed–like cane growing along its banks. Others settled nearby, in the Cane Creek Valley. For many years the entire area was known as the Cane Creek settlement. This extended into what is now Chatham County on the south, and into Randolph County and Guilford County as far as New Garden on the west. The eastern boundary was the Eno River near Hillsborough. Bass's Mountain and Mary's Creek formed the northern boundary (Griffin "History" 3).

At the time the first settlers came to this area, it was part of Bladen or Anson County as identified on the early land grants. In 1752, Orange County was formed and included the Cane Creek settlement. When Chatham County was formed in 1771, the northern boundary line ran just south of the Cane Creek Meeting-house, thus placing the meetinghouse and members who lived north of the line in Orange County, while those living south of the meetinghouse were in Chatham County. Records of many of the early families show the birth of older children in Orange County and the birth of younger children in Chatham County. This leads one to conclude that the families had moved when in reality they had not.

In 1849, Alamance County was formed from western Orange County, putting Cane Creek in Alamance County (Whitaker 89). In 1895, the Chatham County line was redrawn once gain, placing it about three miles south of the meetinghouse (Griffin "History" 15). Therefore, one would be quite accurate in stating that the Cane Creek Meetinghouse has been in Anson or Bladen County, Orange, Chatham, and Alamance counties.

Friends arrived in the Cane Creek area as early as 1749. One of the first acts of business of the newly formed Cane Creek Meeting was to record the births of four children in that year: John

Chamness, son of Anthony and Sarah Cole Chamness; Nathan Pike, tenth child of John and Abigail Overman Pike; Thomas Brown, son of William and Hannah Moon Brown; and Sarah Wright, daughter of John and Rachel Wells Wright.

Since the settlement covered such a wide area it would be impossible to name the thirty families mentioned in the Minutes, but in the immediate Cane Creek area we find these here before 1751: Joseph and Charity Wells, John and Abigail Pike, George Williams, Anthony and Sarah Chamness, William and Hannah Brown, Hugh and Mary Laughlin, Benjamin Martin, William Aldrage, Thomas Jones, Richard Kemp, James Carter, Zachariah Martin, John Tidwell, and John and Rachel Wright.

Land grants in the area were recorded as early as 1749. George Williams' land grant for 645 acres on the north side of Cane Creek was recorded on May 17 of that year. In 1750 two grants were made from the "Earl of Granville's province — Anson or Bladen County." Anthony Chamness was granted 490 acres of land on "Cain Creek" and John Pike was granted 280 acres, also on Cane Creek. John Wright claimed 404 acres on the north side of Cane Creek joining James Williams' property. Four years later in 1754, John Stanfield was granted 203 acres on a branch of Cane Creek. In that same year on May 30, John Jones was granted 632 acres, "lying on a branch of Cain Creek to John Wright's line" (Griffin "History" 2).

Each land grant carried the names of the chain bearers and the surveyors. In all probability these men would have lived in the general area, thus providing a more complete list of settlers' names: Richard Kemp, Martin Aldrage, William Aldrage, James Williams, John Stanfield, William Maris, and William Tidwell (Griffin Notes).

The immigration of the Dixon family followed a typical pattern. "William Dixon or Dixson from Parish of Segoe, County Armagh and other Friends settled on the west side of Brandywine

Creek in Christiana Hundred, New Castle County, near the present village of Centerville and became founders of what later was known as Centre Meeting, New Castle County, Delaware" (Cook). A generation later they would move up the Brandywine to Kennett Square; from there, farther into Pennsylvania and finally southward to the Carolinas within a period of seventy–five years or three generations.

Simon Dixon was one of the first Quaker men to claim land along the Cane Creek. He came to the area, then, in Orange County, in 1749, and chose a spot on the north bank of the creek. There he built a simple cabin, cleared a plot of land for corn, and began plans for a homestead. He did not remain in Carolina at this time but, instead, returned to Pennsylvania. He was most likely traveling with a group of Quaker men. Usually, one man from each family, all of whom were probably neighbors or relatives or members of a certain meeting — ones with the "frontier fever" — went south together on horseback to stake out their claims, then returned north for their families.

Dixon returned to Cane Creek in 1751, clearly intending to stay this time, for he brought his wife Elizabeth, his children, and his widowed mother with him. He also brought provisions for his livelihood: a set of millstones to be used in the mill which he planned to build on Cane Creek. Eventually he would build for his family a stone house, but in the beginning a log cabin would have to suffice. It was not long until he had built a dam across the creek. Soon the mill was built and the millstones installed. When other pieces of equipment were in place, Dixon's Mill was ready for business, and it would serve the community for approximately two centuries.

Anthony and Sarah Cole Chamness may have had the most unusual arrival in the New World and their subsequent settlement in the Cane Creek area. Seth Hinshaw tells of their experiences in

The Carolina Quaker Experience:

One fascinating story of an indentured servant is that of Anthony Chamness. As a boy of thirteen in London, while watching ships on the Thames, he was kidnapped, brought to America, then sold as an indentured servant. During his period of servitude he fell in love with Sarah Cole, an indentured servant girl. In order to hasten her day of liberation, he volunteered to serve part of her remaining time. When at last they were free to get married (ca. 1725) their equipment for housekeeping consisted of a broken wooden bowl which she had found, and a wooden spoon which he had whittled out for her. As soon as possible they moved southward to the Cane Creek area, and joined the meeting. They reared a large family of thirteen children (22).

John and Abigail Pike were two more of the early settlers. Abigail was a minister, and it was not unusual for them to travel to new places and lend their support to the establishment of new Friends communities and meetings. They had left Pasquotank County in eastern North Carolina in 1738 to travel to Frederick County, Virginia, to assist with the Hopewell Meeting, where they remained for eleven years (Griffin "History" 2).

It is possible that the Pikes heard about the new settlement on Cane Creek from families moving into the Hopewell area. Many of these families planned only to remain at Hopewell for a few years, then continue farther south.

John and Abigail came to the Cane Creek settlement with their eight children about 1749. Their certificates of membership from Hopewell were placed with the Carver's Creek Meeting in Bladen County, North Carolina. This monthly meeting held the certificates of not only the Pikes but others in the settlement until the establishment of a monthly meeting at Cane Creek. This was an accepted practice of the day. Many Quaker pioneers, with their staunch faith, did not want to be away from the care of a monthly meeting even if that meeting were many miles away.

Abigail Pike was the archetypal Quaker pioneer woman. Such a woman would of necessity have been strong, in order to cope with the rigors of frontier life. As a minister she would also have been strong in her religious faith and obedient to the leadings of the Holy Spirit. Her concern for the spiritual life of her neighbors would provide opportunities for service which she did not shirk. With Abigail's background, then, it is not surprising that in the early part of the year 1751, she would stand in a meeting for worship and say to the assembled Friends at Cane Creek, "If Rachel Wright will go with me, we will attend the Quarterly Meeting at Little River in Perquimans County and ask that a meeting be set up here." Friends agreed (Griffin "History" 2).

When she set out for the quarterly meeting, Abigail Pike left behind a young son, Nathan, while Rachel Wright also left a small child, Sarah. Both families were large, so the youngsters were not neglected. Moreover, the fact that the children were left by their mothers reveals the determination of both women to fulfill the obligation they had undertaken, as well as the depth of their concern for the spiritual life of the more than thirty families living in the Cane Creek settlement.

Perquimans County lies about two hundred miles to the east of Cane Creek and the trip takes approximately five hours by car now. Imagine the difficulty of traveling that distance on horseback through virtually uncharted wilderness. No doubt there were a few places along the route where a night's lodging and a simple meal could be obtained, but the nights when it was necessary to camp in the open were far more numerous. The Friends at Cane Creek prudently sent other persons with these two courageous women. Their exact number, however, is not known for they are grouped together as "Several friends from them parts" (Crow 2).

17

The establishment of Cane Creek Monthly Meeting of Friends was authorized at the quarterly meeting held at Little River, as recorded in their minutes, dated "Sixth month 31st,"[1] 1751:

> Friends on Cane Creek wrote to our Quarterly Meeting Desiring a Monthly Meeting to be Settled amongst them which was Refer'd to this Meeting, & Several Friends from them parts appeared at this Meeting & acquainted Friends that there is Thirty Families and upwards of Friends Settled in them parts, and Desire in behalf of themselves and their Friends to have a Monthly Meeting Settled amongst them, which Request, upon Mature Consideration Friends think it proper to grant, and leave to themselves to settle it in the most convenient place amongst the body (Crow 3).

Now would begin the long trek back. The hot September sun would make travel more uncomfortable, and there would be the incessant insects with which to contend. But the good news Abigail Pike, Rachel Wright, and the others carried with them would lessen the difficulties. How happy the day of return must have been, not only for the families of those returning, but for the entire group of Quakers settled along the banks of Cane Creek. At last they would have a monthly meeting of their own, and no longer would their certificates of membership be held by a faraway monthly meeting.

Abigail Pike's story does not end with the establishment of the meeting at Cane Creek. She was also involved in the effort to secure a monthly meeting for Friends at New Garden, and the mere thirty–five miles she traveled in that endeavor must have been as

---

[1] This date was in "Old Style," due to the fact that the British Empire, including the American colonies, did not adopt the Gregorian calendar reforms until September 1752. Before that time, the year began with March, so that "Sixth Month" in the date above refers to August, not June. "Sixth Month 31st, 1751," would correspond to September 11, 1751 on our modern calendar.

nothing compared to the journey she had made on behalf of Cane Creek. Her efforts were again successful, for New Garden Meeting was established shortly after the one at Cane Creek. By 1775, Abigail, now widowed, would request and receive transfer of her membership to New Garden.

At the first monthly meeting held at Cane Creek Tenth month 1751, fifteen certificates were presented for membership: John Powell; Martha Hiatt and children; John Hiatt; Joseph Doan; Robert Summers with his wife and children; Simon Dixon; Aaron Jones; Henry Ballenger with his wife and children; William Reynolds with his wife and children; and Elizabeth Vestal and her two sons, William and Thomas. During the first year of the Cane Creek Meeting, sixty–eight certificates were received and approved. These early settlers of the community called Cane Creek had proven themselves to be strong, God–fearing people. In just a few years they had built their homes, provided for their livelihoods, and established a monthly meeting which continues to this day (Griffin "History" 3).

House built by John Allen, who moved from London Grove, Pennsylvania, to the Cane Creek community in 1749. Picture ca. 1882.

EARLY LAND GRANTS

A generalization (not drawn to scale)

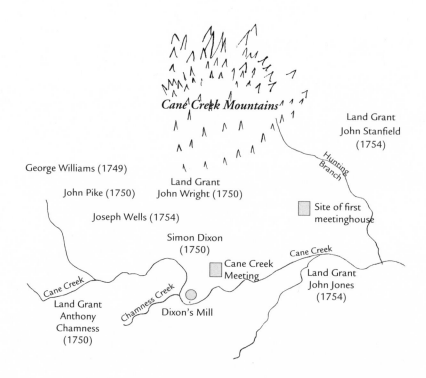

MOTHER OF MEETINGS

Today, Cane Creek Monthly Meeting con-
sists of one meetinghouse and one congregation, with most members living within
a few miles of each other and the meetinghouse.
This has not always been so. The organization of
early Friends in North America was patterned after
the system of organization still in use among British Friends (Smith 41). Under this system, a
monthly meeting would consist of a number of
preparative meetings on a fairly permanent basis.
Each preparative meeting would prepare business
pertinent to its area, which would then be for-
warded to the monthly meeting for consideration.
Each preparative meeting was also required to send
a representative to the monthly meeting for busi-

ness, and, should it fail to do so, someone would be appointed to inquire into the reason for the absence.

In the early years the members of Cane Creek Meeting were scattered over piedmont North Carolina from New Garden in the west to Eno, near Hillsborough, in the east. This created much hardship for the faithful Quakers who had to travel long distances to meetings for worship and also to monthly business meetings. Therefore, it is not surprising that at the first monthly meeting for business at Cane Creek, held Tenth month 1751, the Minutes state that Friends of New Garden requested "the privilege of holding a meeting for worship in that place." In just three months they would be granted the privilege of holding a preparative meeting. By 1754, New Garden had grown strong enough to be granted monthly meeting status, thus becoming the first of many meetings in this area with roots in Cane Creek Monthly Meeting. Having their own monthly meeting saved New Garden Friends the inconvenience of a thirty–mile ride on horseback to attend meetings for business at Cane Creek.

Another early group who wanted to begin their own meeting was not so far away. In 1754, it is recorded in the April Minutes that Friends at Rocky River requested permission to hold a meeting for worship for those persons "inhabiting along the banks of Rocky River." This permission was given, and today the Rocky River Meetinghouse is located in Chatham County about five miles south of Cane Creek.

The monthly meeting's business sessions might rotate or circulate among the meetinghouses of the preparative meetings. This would more evenly distribute the difficulties of early travel among the membership. Cane Creek Monthly Meeting circulated its business meetings among the preparative meetings when feasible. New Garden and Cane Creek rotated the monthly meeting until 1754, when New Garden was granted monthly meeting status. At monthly meeting held Twelfth month 1820, Friends at Rocky River requested that Cane Creek Monthly Meeting hold its meeting for business once in every two months at the Rocky River Meetinghouse. This was agreeable, and, in February 1821, Cane Creek Monthly Meeting for business was held at Rocky River. This practice continued until Rocky River Monthly Meeting was established in 1908. As late as 1902, Cane Creek Monthly Meeting also held two meetings yearly with Edward Hill Meeting "whenever it was thought best."

It is interesting to note that there was a Cane Creek preparative meeting also. This was done, not in preparation for attaining monthly meeting status (for that was already accomplished), but rather to take care of matters of concern for the immediate area of Cane Creek. It is not at all unusual to read in the monthly meeting Minutes that "Cane Creek preparative complained of . . . ." followed by a person's name and the offense committed.

Cane Creek Monthly Meeting eagerly met the challenge of establishing new meetings. Not only were Cane Creek Friends willing to establish these new meetings but they also assumed responsibility for their care and oversight. In 1757, William Reckett, a friend who traveled throughout the colonies, visited Cane Creek and recorded in his journal,

> There is a large body of Friends gathered together in a few years from several provinces. They told me they had settled there about ten years but had found occasion to build five meetinghouses and wanted one or two more. I had good and reasonable opportunities with them (Weeks 103).

There is some confusion about the number of meetings begun by Cane Creek. In some cases records have been lost, while in others the existing records are not clear. The Cane Creek Minutes are brief and factual with little elaboration regarding the business transacted. Through the years some names have been lost or changed. However, the meetings which might be regarded as the "children" of Cane Creek fall into three categories: those which still exist and are still active today, those that were "laid down," and those whose beginnings were helped or supported by Friends from other monthly meetings.

In addition to New Garden and Rocky River, five other meetings begun by Cane Creek are still active: Centre, Holly Spring, Deep River, Spring, and Edward Hill. A sixth, Back Creek, received from Cane Creek its initial permission for an indulged meeting for worship but would later be established as a monthly meeting by Centre.

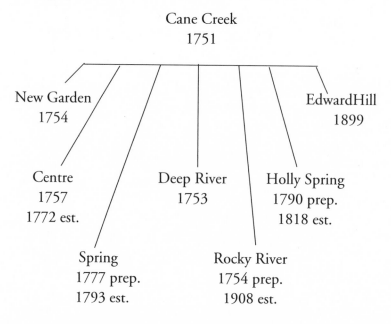

Cane Creek
1751

New Garden
1754

EdwardHill
1899

Centre
1757
1772 est.

Deep River
1753

Holly Spring
1790 prep.
1818 est.

Spring
1777 prep.
1793 est.

Rocky River
1754 prep.
1908 est.

Centre began meeting for worship in 1757, and in 1772, Cane Creek gave permission for them to become a separate monthly meeting (Griffin "History" 16). Centre Meeting is located on Highway 62 in Guilford County. It took its name, Centre, because it was located approximately halfway between Cane Creek and New Garden Meetings.

The minutes of Cane Creek Monthly Meeting dated Eleventh month 1753 record that "Friends of Deep River requested to hold a meeting for worship among themselves every other Fifth day [Thursday] at the home of Thomas Mills." Thus, Deep River Monthly Meeting began. Deep River is located in Guilford County in the High Point area.

Five miles to the east of Cane Creek, a group of Friends received permission to hold an "indulged meeting" on First days in 1764 (Cane Creek Minutes April 1764). An indulged meeting is one for which a request has been made to have a meeting for worship and this request has been granted or indulged. Thirteen years later, in 1777, this group was given permission to have a preparative meeting. Monthly meeting status was attained in 1793 by Spring Meeting.

Begun late in the nineteenth century, Edward Hill was Cane Creek's last successful attempt to begin a new meeting. Edward Hill was started in 1899 and is located in Chatham County near the small town of Bonlee.

Back Creek Meeting was begun in 1785 when Cane Creek Meeting approved an indulged meeting for worship. Sometime later, however, the people who had the concern for a meeting at Back Creek transferred their membership from Cane Creek to Centre Meeting. Their concern was then handled by the Centre Meeting rather than Cane Creek. At Western Quarterly Meeting, held at Cane Creek Eleventh month 1792, Back Creek was granted the status of monthly meeting. Today the meetinghouse is located to the west of Asheboro in Randolph County.

Eight of the meetings begun by Cane Creek have been "laid down" or discontinued. As the region became more populated, some meetings were absorbed by more rapidly growing meetings. Sometimes the interest and support for a meeting would decline, but whatever the reason, no meeting was ever laid down without much consideration.

The Pee Dee Meeting was started in 1755 and was located in Lancaster County, South Carolina, on the Little Pee Dee River. From the Minutes of Cane Creek Monthly Meeting, Ninth month 1755, "Friends on the Pee Dee request for meeting for worship on first and fourth days, where as customary care was extended a committee was appointed to visit Pee Dee." Two months later, permission was granted. William Reckett, in the account of his travels to the early meetings, found this meeting to be one whose "love to truth and dilligence in attending meetings are worthy of notice; for they had nigh one hundred miles to go to the monthly meeting they belonged to, and I am informed very seldom missed attending" (Weeks 113). The travel was not one–way only, for, according to the Minutes of First month 1779, Joseph Cloud and John Carter were given permission by Cane Creek Monthly Meeting to visit Pee Dee.

The meeting was laid down around 1799. No reason is given in the minutes of Cane Creek, but in that year there was decline of meetings in South Carolina and Georgia. Joseph Cloud visited the area again at this time presumably in the "interest of removal" (Weeks 123, 124). However, the Cane Creek Minutes of June 1799, reveal that Friends from Pee Dee petitioned the monthly meeting to have their rights removed to Deep River in 1799. Could it be that their request precipitated Joseph Cloud's visit, or could it be that the request came after his visit to Pee Dee?

The decade between 1830–1840 saw the demise of several meetings begun by Cane Creek. Little is known about several of them. Friends from Lower Deep River requested the privilege of holding a meeting on Fifth day, 1763. This meeting continued until 1837 when it was laid down. Trotter's Creek was also laid down in 1837. This meeting was located in the southeast corner of Guilford County. Brush Creek, located south of Tick Creek, held meetings from 1796 until 1830. This meeting was later known as the Ridge. There was a meeting located south of Siler City, near Glendon, known as Napton Meeting. This meeting was established in 1780 and continued until 1836. Cane Creek Monthly Meeting received $30.00 for sale of the Ridge Meetinghouse, but there is no record of what happened to the Napton Meetinghouse. Older Friends say it was used for a school until about the turn of the century.

Mill Creek Meeting was located in Cox's Settlement in an area which later became Randolph County, some twenty miles from Cane Creek. Little is known about its beginnings, but some meetings were probably held in the home of William Cox, who built Cox's Mill on Mill Creek. Friends in the area formally requested the privilege of holding meetings for worship in 1758. Cane Creek finally sent a committee to examine the situation, and a favorable report was given in 1760. The Cane Creek Minutes do not state the reason, but the privilege of holding meetings for worship was suspended temporarily in 1765. There is no further word for several years, but in the meantime the Quaker population of the area had shifted south and west, with some Friends living as far as Upper Richland Creek, seven miles away. Consequently a meetinghouse was built and a cemetery started at a location called Holly Spring. This meeting was granted the status of Preparative Meeting in 1790, and Monthly Meeting in 1818.

Sandy Creek Meeting was begun in 1780. In June of that year, these Friends asked for the privilege of holding meetings for worship on "First and week days." This request was granted with the exception noted, "except First day of Quarterly Meeting and Fifth day of week at Cane Creek." The meeting was located in

Randolph County, west of Liberty, for about fifteen years. In 1788, Cane Creek Monthly Meeting was asked for advice about "setting up another meeting place, being deprived of former house." A committee was appointed to advise and assist them, but unfortunately no record was made of the outcome. This gives rise to an unanswered question: why were they deprived of a meeting place?

Herman Husband owned a large tract of land in that area. Whether or not the influence of his Quaker beliefs had anything to do with the establishment of the meeting is quite uncertain but perhaps plausible. Husband, himself, was not in the area after 1771. Seth Hinshaw, in his book *Friends at Holly Spring*, attributes the demise of Sandy Creek to strong Baptist evangelism and migrations westward (16).

Tyson's Meeting was started in 1783 on Deep River in Chatham County near Carbonton. A group of Friends reported to the monthly meeting Sixth month 1800 that they had "visited families of Friends near Tyson's and in their judgement it would be best to discontinue the indulgence of the meeting." The basis of their judgment is unknown.

Dunn's Creek, located "on the Cape Fear," was begun in 1746. William Reckett also visited this meeting but found it to be "a small gathering . . . but had been much hurt and scattered in their minds from the true shepherd" (Weeks 91). Originally, this meeting was connected to Eastern Quarterly Meeting, but in 1760, it was joined to the newly formed Western Quarterly Meeting of North Carolina Yearly Meeting. It was probably at this time that Cane Creek became actively involved in supporting and encouraging the Friends at Dunn's Creek. However, their interest and help was not enough because the meeting was laid down in 1772. This was the first monthly meeting to be laid down within limits of the North Carolina Yearly Meeting (Weeks 102).

In April of 1815, Long's Mill Meeting was begun near Long's Mill on the banks of Cane Creek. Two months prior to this, Friends living in the area of Long's Mill had asked that they be allowed to hold a meeting "amongst themselves." After the traditional visit of a committee, Cane Creek Monthly Meeting granted their request. By 1820, Long's Mill Meeting felt that they were ready to become a preparative meeting, but Cane Creek Monthly Meeting did not agree and their request for preparative status was denied, as stated in the Minutes of August 1820. Just how long this group continued to meet is unknown.

Hedgecock's Creek Meeting was in Chatham County, but the exact location of the meeting is unknown. However, there is a Hedgecock's Creek in the general area of Bonlee. Perhaps these friends did as so many of the early Friends had done; they built their meetinghouse near the creek and chose to name their meeting accordingly. The date for its establishment is not known, but it was laid down in 1805 (Griffin Notes).

A small number of the meetings which Cane Creek set up as preparative meetings were taken under the care of another established meeting. For example, in 1880, Cane Creek began a preparative meeting in Moore County near High Falls (Griffin Notes). It was called Prosperity. Later, this meeting would be under the care of Holly Spring Meeting, and it was during this later time that Prosperity Monthly Meeting was established.

Information is very scarce concerning the meeting referred to as Dixon's which was laid down in 1805 (Weeks 336). There is no indication of the location. Tradition says that Simon Dixon had a second mill east of the one near Cane Creek Meeting. Could it be that Dixon's Meeting was close to that mill? This is another unanswered question. Stephen B. Weeks attributes the beginning of this meeting to Spring, but tradition attributes it to Cane Creek (336).

There was also an early meeting at Eno, near Hillsborough. These Friends were charter members of Cane Creek. In fact, there may have been a settlement at Eno before the one at Cane Creek, as there were meetings for worship in that area by 1751. In 1761, a preparative meeting was begun (Newlin 137).

Friends at Eno seem to have had an independent spirit somewhat apart from the Quaker mainstream of their time. They did not always conform to what was expected of them. A minute from the women's monthly business meeting, Sixth month 1767, provides the information that a committee of three women was appointed to visit Eno because "they did not attend mid–week meeting." The committee was to "visit them and bring them to a sense of their disorderly conduct." They reported that they had found a lukewarm situation at Eno and recommended the privilege of holding a meeting be taken away. There are other, similar incidents recorded. In July 1767, the Minutes indicate that a different committee was appointed to "stir them up to more diligence in attending meetings for discipline or whatever else they might find."

Eventually Eno would become a subordinate of Spring Meeting. By 1847, it became necessary to lay down the meeting (Newlin 137). The site of the Eno Meeting was one mile north of Hillsborough on the Eno River in Orange County.

Graham Friends Meeting was organized by Western Quarterly Meeting in 1907. Cane Creek helped in that endeavor (Griffin Notes).

There are no preparative meetings under the care of Cane Creek Monthly Meeting at the present time. The last direct effort on the part of Cane Creek to begin a new meeting was an attempt in Burlington in the 1970s, which was undertaken in conjunction with the other meetings in Western Quarter. This was a second attempt to establish a meeting there; the first was in 1893 (Weeks

335). Neither attempt was successful. Cane Creek has also given monetary support to the North Carolina Yearly Meeting's effort to begin a meeting in the Raleigh area at the present time.

Cane Creek Monthly Meeting has been affectionately called the "Mother of Meetings." This is an apt title, for one cannot travel far in the realm of North Carolina Quakerism without encountering one of her "offspring."

BURYING GROUND

The Cane Creek cemetery crowds the meetinghouse as if in death those who lie there seek comfort and help, much as they did in life. Here lie representatives of several of the colonies. England, Ireland, Scotland, and Germany are also represented. Soldiers from the Regulator Movement, as well as every war in which our country has been involved, lie here. British soldiers mortally wounded at the Battle of Guilford Court House, who died during Lord Cornwallis' encampment nearby, found a resting place here. The well–to–do and the poor sleep side by side. It has been said that slaves as well as free black people were buried around the edges of the cemetery. If so, their graves have since been lost or were left unmarked.

Tradition says that the first burial was that of a child whose family was passing through the area. While they were camped here, the child died. With sadness, the father dug a grave, wrapped the child in a blanket, took the feed trough from the wagon, and used it as a coffin. After burying the child, the family moved on. No date is given for this burial. However, the earliest dated stone in the cemetery bears the mark "M"— 1752. Could that be the child? Perhaps others were buried earlier in unmarked graves, but the earliest marked stone is that of Ruth Dixon Doan — 1764. Joel Brooks's death and burial were recorded in the monthly meeting Minutes of Ninth month 1764. No marker for his grave can be located.

Adhering to the Quaker belief in simplicity, many of the older graves are marked with small field stones bearing only an initial and a date. Sometimes there is only a date. Friends kept careful records of births and deaths that provide valuable information today. However, the graves of many non–members are lost.

There are many vacant areas in the old cemetery where un-

A part of the old section of Cane Creek Cemetery

Jesse Dixon (1784–1873)

marked graves are located. In 1828, the yearly meeting forbade the use of "manufactured stones," and a committee visited each cemetery to see that such stones were removed (Griffin "History" 10). The order must have been rescinded later or the monthly meeting chose to disregard it, as shown by the kinds of stones over most of the graveyard. It is said that Jesse Dixon (1784–1873) selected a stone, carved his birth date, and asked his brother to put his death date on it and place it at his grave.

A walk through the cemetery reveals many interesting and unusual markers. Prompted by the Historical Society of Southern Alamance County, whose purpose was honoring pioneer families, Cane Creek Monthly Meeting planned to hold annual reunions of the descendants of its founding fathers. During each reunion a grave marker would be unveiled in honor of one of the pioneer settlers.

Dedication of Simon Dixon's grave marker, 1925.

The first reunion was held in October 1925, and a marker fashioned from a millstone was placed at the grave of Simon Dixon (1728–1781) and his wife, Elizabeth Allen Dixon (1728–1793). In August 1926, a marker was unveiled for John Allen, a pioneer teacher. A year later, the Stuart family placed a marker for their ancestor, Alexander Stuart, a farmer. Appropriately, a sickle was embedded in this marker (Griffin "History" 11).

John and Abigail Overman Pike were honored in 1928. Both were leaders and "weighty" Friends[1] during their lifetimes. After

---

[1]"Weighty" Friends are those whose opinions and counsel carried more weight in the meeting due to merit.

the death of her husband, Abigail Pike left Cane Creek and went to Muddy Creek, near Deep River, to live with her son. She died and was buried there in February of 1781. The cemetery of this meeting still exists on the outskirts of the present town of Kernersville in Forsyth County, and the grave which is thought to be Abigail's is outlined with handmade brick. Thus, the marker at Cane Creek honors her memory, not her actual grave.

William and Rebecca Dixon Marshall were honored in 1929. Their marker records their gift of land for the meetinghouse. Later on, the Stout family honored Peter Stout, affectionately called the "Quaker," and his wife, Margaret Cypert Stout. He had sat "at the head of the Meeting" for many years, as well as serving in many other capacities.

In 1941, a British flag flew once again at Cane Creek. This time the flag was a gift; it was sent by the King of England, George VI. The Saxapahaw Boy Scouts, Troop 46, unveiled a marker erected to the memory of the British soldiers who were buried in the cemetery in 1781. The original marker was a large field stone with the dedication plaque attached. However, soon after the dedication a large millstone was found and the plaque was transferred to it

Members of the Saxapahaw Boy Scouts, Troop 46, in 1941,
unveiling the marker erected in memory of the British soldiers
who were buried in the cemetery in 1781. Boy on left: Albert Cheek.

(Griffin "History" 11). The millstone was embedded in a large concrete block and is about five feet tall. The inscription on the stone reads, "A memorial to British Troops who died in the Old Meeting house during Cornwallis' encampment here on his retreat from Guilford Court House March 1781. Erected by troop 46 B.S.A. Henry Overman leader, who died before completing it."

No doubt the kind of program for each marker dedication was different. A typical program was probably very much like the one for the Dixon–Marshall reunion on August 16, 1930. On that day the program began at 10:30 A.M. with a welcome by the president of the Historical Society, E. P. Dixon. A period of silent worship followed. The audience participated in song. Then R. H. Hutchison, a local historian, told the story of the Marshall family. After another song, the pastor of Cane Creek, Lewis McFarland, unveiled and dedicated the marker. A picnic lunch was served at noon. The afternoon was reserved for a social hour or hours.

After the first few years, membership and interest in the historical society waned and the practice of erecting markers to honor certain families was discontinued. However, some forty years later in 1973, Hannah Hadley Dixon Stanfield was honored by her descendants. The last pioneer family to be honored was that of Anthony and Sarah Cole Chamness, in 1975. Both of these markers were given and erected by family members and not by any organization.

Today one can walk among the simple rocks and stones and envision those early Friends. More elaborate stones mark the graves of those who have been interred in more recent years. A sense of history and peace pervades this place which has seen much sorrow in its 240 years.

TRAVELING FRIENDS

One factor enormously important in the religious life of early Friends in North Carolina was the visits of traveling Friends. This was a unique ministry practiced faithfully and prayerfully by many early Friends, even those who had to cross seas.

The isolation of the wilderness would have been much harder to endure had it not been for the life–giving visits of Friends who traveled, under a concern, to the remote places where other Friends had settled. These people brought more than encouragement and inspiration. Traveling ministers brought instruction to Friends who were far removed from the mainstream of the Quaker movement and who needed information and guidance in the proper conduct of their meetings and daily lives. Considering the hardships of travel at the time, it is truly amazing to know of the large number of Friends who came to Cane Creek and the large number of visits undertaken by members of Cane Creek to distant places as well.

When the visitors arrived at their destinations, they attended any public meetings that were held, either monthly meetings or meetings for worship. At that time they would share "what God had laid on their hearts" with the members of the meeting. Their visitations were not limited to the public meetings, however. The travelers would also visit families and individuals, if necessary, to carry out their charges. There would be time to pray together and talk together, as well as meditate and rejoice together.

It must have been an exciting time in the settlements when such visitors came. Arrangements would have to be made for their accommodations. Usually there would be two or three in the party, sometimes more. Early homes were small but visitors were cordially welcomed. In some cases the family may have had to double up — or triple up — on their normal sleeping arrangements, but this would have been done gladly, for visitors brought glimpses of other Friends and relieved the isolation of many families.

Cane Creek Minutes mention numerous visits of concerned Friends. One of the earliest was that of Catherine Phillips, an English Friend, in December 1753. She tells of her visit in her memoirs:

> On the 29th we got to cane Creek, another new settlement of Friends with whom we had a meeting the 30th wherein we were rather low, yet favored with peace in our spirits.

On the thirty–first she arrived at Eno, then on

> 2nd day of 1st month 1754. My companion, Mary Peisley, returned to Cane Creek to be at the week day meeting. I

returned to Cane Creek on the fourth. Same day we had a meeting at Rocky River and was satisfactory and returned to Cane Creek for First Day Meeting. On the 7th we left for Carver's Creek. Jeremiah and John Wright accompanied us (Griffin "History" 18).

From the Cane Creek Minutes we read that

Friend Mary Kirby accompanied by Grace Crosdale of Pennsylvania on 3rd of 3rd month 1759, Rachel Wilson of old England with Sarah Jenny of Virginia 7th of 1st month 1769.

These names are only a very few of the hundreds who visited in the early years. Almost without exception their visits were recorded as inspirational and uplifting.

Some of the visitors were not very complimentary. Consider a report from John Griffith's journal, 1765:

The meeting at Cane Creek is very large, but most members seem void of solid sense and solemnity, a spirit of self–righteousness and contention was felt. Went to their First Day Meeting, but there was much darkness and death over them. The leaven of the Pharisees seemed to prevail (Weeks 112).

Cane Creek Meeting not only recorded visits; the members of the meeting often felt led to visit and attend other meetings in the "Service of Truth." A search of the Cane Creek Monthly Meeting Minutes reveals that Rachel Wright traveled in the lower parts of Virginia with Hannah Ballinger in July 1752, and Abigail Pike and Mary Jones visited the meeting at Thomas Pugh's later that same year. Joseph Cloud made many visits in the years between 1779 and 1804 to Tyson's Settlement, to "Friends on the Western Waters," to eastern Pennsylvania, and to Europe in 1804. Other visitors from Cane Creek included John Carter, Mincher Litler, and Zachariah Dicks.

Sometimes the meeting would give specific instructions for the visits. For example, in Sixth month 1767, a committee of three women was appointed to visit the Eno Meeting

> and bring them to a sense of their disorderly conduct; also to visit all the branches of Cane Creek Meeting to stir them up to more diligence in attending meetings for discipline, or whatever else is needed. . . .

One of the women who made many visits as she served her meeting was Abigail Overman Pike. She and her husband were charter members of Cane Creek Meeting and served it diligently for many years. Abigail was also a Friends minister. Tradition says that it was in that capacity that she would ride out to the army camps and preach to the soldiers. It is not clear which army allowed her to preach. As in all things the retelling of stories often blurs the events. It is possible that it could have been both the British and the American forces. Abigail transferred her membership from Cane. Creek to New Garden in 1775. One could assume that the events told here could have happened near the time of the Battle of Guilford Court House and the Battle of New Garden. It is not likely that she would have been intimidated by either the British or the Americans. General Nathanael Greene, himself a Quaker at one time, may have endorsed her ministry, because she was said to be the only minister allowed within the lines. She was not allowed to dismount; therefore, her sermons were preached from horseback.

One night while returning from such a visit, Abigail met friends along the way, and soon they came to where the road divided. One fork of the road led straight home, and the other led past the graveyard. They debated which way to go; one remarked that a ghost could be seen in the graveyard. Abigail whipped up her horse saying, "We will go this way then, I have long wanted to see a ghost, shake hands with it and ask, 'Is it well with thee?'" When they arrived at the cemetery, there did appear to be a ghost standing with arms outstretched as though welcoming them. Unafraid, Abigail rode up to it and called back, "Come on friends, it is only a big cobweb on a bush."

Another story which has been passed down through the generations tells of her pitcher. Abigail had a set of "Queensware" porcelain china dishes. These were very rare in those days, particularly in a backwoods cabin. One day British soldiers came to her cabin searching for food and overturned her cupboard. She tried to catch some of the dishes in her outstretched apron but was only able to save one small pitcher. That pitcher was passed down through the years from one daughter to another and was last reported in a museum in Oklahoma in 1975. What a story that pitcher could tell!

The ministry of visiting Friends has vanished almost completely. As with so many other things, something meaningful has passed from the scene.

FIVE MEETINGHOUSES

Although Cane Creek Monthly Meeting was not organized until 1751, one may be sure that early Friends established meetings for worship in their homes, as all Friends did just as soon as they settled. The first meetinghouse was probably made of logs, as that was the accepted and available building material at that time. It would have been large enough to seat a small number of people, the men on one side and the women on the other. As was the custom of Friends meetinghouses, there would have been a facing bench across the front of the meeting room for the use of elders, ministers, overseers, and invited guests. This first meetinghouse stood near the center of the Cane Creek settlement, about one mile east of the location of the present meetinghouse. It was north of the Cane Creek, on or near the farm of the late Lawrence McPherson. The unmarked site is near the Snow Camp intersection, about one and a half miles north on North Carolina State Road 1004. The meetinghouse would have stood on the far side of the field, to the right of the road at that point.

The meetinghouse was located on a portion of land which was a part of the land grant of John Stanfield. In his will, dated August 4, 1755, he willed a parcel of land including the "meetinghouse lot" to his son Thomas. By the early 1900s the Thomas Stanfield land belonged to John Thompson. His will, dated 1907, states:

> To my four living sons and their heirs, Simeon, David, Jonathan, and William Jesse, all my real estate consisting of homeplace, fifty–two acres, two Marshall places — 156 acres, and a lot known as the meetinghouse lot.

The heirs divided the property and William Jesse's part included the meetinghouse lot. Today the McPherson farm includes the land which belonged to William Jesse Thompson (Griffin "History" 4).

In 1764, William and Rebecca Marshall gave twenty–six acres of land and "the house on it" to be used for the meeting. It is not clear if this house was made into the second meetinghouse for Cane Creek or if a new meetinghouse was built on the property. If a new building was constructed, it seems reasonable that it would have been a log meetinghouse similar to the first one. Tradition says that this second meetinghouse stood east of the present building, near the center of the cemetery. How long this building was used is not known, but it is recorded that it underwent renovation and extensive repairs in the late 1780s. At a monthly meeting held Ninth month 1786, a communication was read from the yearly meeting committee for Western Quarterly Meeting. It stated that John Townsend and Mark Reaves, from Ireland, had visited

Southern Friends and that they had found meetinghouses in "disrepair in remote places . . . some scarcely fit to hold meetings in." They felt that this was caused by the "difficulties and straitened circumstances to which Friends have been reduced by the calamities of war." These two men had given £200 in Pennsylvania currency to help those meetings least able to repair their meetinghouses. They further instructed that there should be a "proper number of windows glazed with glass to give light and there should be shutters." The members of the monthly meeting agreed to use their "best endeavor to repair and put in order the meetinghouse agreeable to the above."

At the time of William and Rebecca Marshall's gift to Cane Creek in the 1760s, the British government forbade anyone to give land for a church except to the Church of England, so the deed for the land was made to four members of the meeting: Peter Stout, Benjamin Piggot, William Piggot, and David Vestal. In 1798, the North Carolina General Assembly gave churches the right to hold property. However, it was not until 1801 that Cane Creek's land was deeded to the trustees of the meeting. The amount of land held by the meeting was reduced in 1807, when the Marshalls' son, John, asked the meeting to sell him ten acres of his parents' original land gift. The meeting agreed and the money received was used to make some repairs on the meetinghouse (Griffin "History" 5).

In the early 1800s, a third meetinghouse was built. Probably by this time, the log structure was again in need of extensive repairs and the growth of the population demanded more space. The prudent Quakers would have concluded that it would be better to build anew than to spend money on the old structure, although the benches from the earlier meetinghouse were used again. The new building was a typical meetinghouse of its time. The façade was made of brick up to the height of the windows, and above that was frame. It was partitioned through the center in order to allow the

46

men and women to meet separately for their business sessions, as was then customary among Friends. A facing bench extended across the front of the meeting room, as was also usual. The new meetinghouse, however, was said to have a heating system, which was very unusual for that time. This building burned in January, 1879. There was some speculation that the heating system may have caused the fire, but its exact cause was never determined (Griffin "History" 5).

Soon after the fire a committee consisting of Samuel Allen, Hugh Dixon, Solomon Dixon, William Henley, and Louis Hornaday was appointed to solicit subscriptions for a new building. A year later this committee reported that it had received between $500 and $600 in subscriptions and that the meetinghouse was so nearly completed that an additional $100 would finish it. This would be the fourth meetinghouse for Cane Creek. It was a large frame building forty feet wide and sixty–seven feet long, with an eighteen–foot ceiling. There was a ministers' gallery extending across the front. The windows along both sides of the interior were quite tall. These were painted white and had dark green outside shutters. Another feature was an elevated floor which was slanted toward the front. There were two aisles in the meetinghouse with longer benches in the middle section. Two sets of shorter benches were on either side of the pulpit at right angles to the main section of benches. One set was known as the choir corner, and the other was known as the amen corner.

Just before the building was finished, the Philadelphia Meeting for Sufferings gave $500 from the Charleston Fund toward the construction, with the provision that as much of the money as necessary should be used to install a moveable or sliding partition through the center of the building. This condition was accepted by the monthly meeting.

In March 1880, meeting for worship was held in the new

The fourth meetinghouse, 1880–1942

building for the first time, and it served the Cane Creek congregation until Sunday, January 4, 1942, when fire again destroyed the meetinghouse. Just as people were gathering for Sunday School, the fire was discovered. Flames roared quickly through the building and nothing was saved except the piano and a few chairs. Once again there was speculation that a faulty heating system might have been the culprit, but no exact cause for the fire was determined. While the coals were still smouldering, a prayer service was held on the front lawn.

The members decided to hold a meeting later in the day at Sylvan School to begin plans for rebuilding. At the afternoon meeting a building committee was appointed. It was made up of Elbert Newlin (the pastor), Jesse Thompson, Claude Coble, Walter

Thomas, James Henley, Lorraine Griffin, and Ruth Moon. Sunday services would be held at nearby Sylvan School until the new building could be completed.

Work was soon started on the brick building which would be Cane Creek's fifth meetinghouse, the one in use today. Throughout the nine months of rebuilding, donations were received from many sources: people with ties to Cane Creek, Friends from across the yearly meeting, other church congregations, businesses, and the membership of Cane Creek itself. Local building supply stores were generous with gifts of materials, some free and some at reduced prices. People with building skills offered their services, while others helped by keeping materials ready and handy for the workers.

In their final report to the monthly meeting, the building committee explained:

> Paul P. Thompson had the brick contract at $8.50 per thousand for the labor. He directed this work up to the main floor, then he went into government work, and Morris Roach became the brick foreman and finished the building.
>
> Charlie Stout was the carpenter foreman at 55¢ per hour, and we are grateful to him for his fine cooperation and excellent work.

There was also payment for the labor of both man and beast: thirty cents was allowed for a workman's labor, and fifteen cents per hour for a team of horses (Griffin "History" 7).

The meetinghouse was dedicated on Homecoming Day, October 6, 1942. On the morning of the dedication, there remained a debt of $1,772.19 to be paid on the building. At the beginning of the service, the pastor, Elbert Newlin, explained the situation and asked for pledges. The congregation responded with great

Cane Creek Meetinghouse, 1942

fervor and in a brief time the building was debt–free (Griffin "History" 6).

There are no exact figures available for the total cost of the building, but it would probably have been somewhere between $30,000 and $35,000. Compare this with the $1,050 the meeting-house cost in the 1780s. Of course, the cost of building materials and furnishings was much less then. One example of the differences in costs may be seen in the previous building committee's report, dating from 1880. The earlier committee reported the purchase of two stovepipes with one knee for $21.15; 1,540 feet of lumber at $20.79; labor for thirty–eight benches at $32.55; nails and screws for $8.40; six chairs at $6.00; four bracket lamps and chimneys at $4.25; and five tables at $10.00 (Griffin "History" 8).

A unique feature of the present building was the water arrange-ment made with Jim Dixon, who lived just across the road from the meetinghouse. The meeting put a water pump into Mr. Dixon's well, with the understanding that he would pay for its operating costs and any repairs that might be necessary. If he should sell the property, the meeting would retain the water rights. Mr. Dixon did not want any money for the use of his well, only the benefit of using the pump for his own water supply (Griffin "History" 7).

The water arrangement with the Dixons has long been obsolete, and with its passing went a tradition for the young people. It was their custom after an evening service to stroll across the road to "Mr. Jim's" for a drink of water. This provided an opportunity for couples to do a little "hand holding" on the way over and back.

Hardy Slate and Cora Lee Gibson in Quaker dress
for the Bicentennial Celebration, 1951

51

Changes have been made to both the interior and the exterior of the meetinghouse through the years. In the late 1960s, services were once again held in Sylvan School while a front porch and steps were added to the building. Also at that time, a walkway around the basement was installed, as well as new classrooms, a pastor's study, and a small kitchen in the basement. A ramp was added to the north entrance to provide access for the elderly and the handicapped.

In 1984, fire once again threatened the building. This time, fortunately, the fire was discovered quickly and only minor damage resulted. The meetinghouse did, however, require a new coat of paint and new carpeting.

Through the years, there have been memorial gifts which have added to the comfort and beauty of the meetinghouse. Cushions for the benches were given in memory of Lester and Olive Allen by their son, George Allen. Pulpit chairs were given by Plato Stuart of Phoenix, Arizona, in memory of his parents, Burton and Emma Stuart. The electrically lighted sign on the front lawn was given by Della Stuart in memory of her husband, Plato. Bibles for the pews were given by Lu and Carl Longest.

Today the meetinghouse is cooled in summer and heated in winter quite comfortably, and sometimes it is easy to forget that these conveniences have not always been available. For example, in 1920, a committee was appointed to install electric lights in the meetinghouse even though electricity was not available in rural areas at that time. A thirty–two volt storage battery was purchased and the building was wired. The initial cost was $155.77, and the monthly bill was eighty cents. This system served the meeting until 1935, when Duke Power extended their lines into the area (Griffin "History" 9).

The facilities of the meeting expanded with the completion of the fellowship building in 1980. It is located to the rear of the meetinghouse. Carpentry students from Southern Alamance High School, under the direction of William Coble, did much of the woodwork, greatly reducing the cost of the building. Thus, through donations and careful stewardship of funds, the building was debt–free when it was ready for use.

There is another small building at the back of the meetinghouse which houses the big pot used for making Brunswick stew, the sale of which has greatly contributed to meeting the building needs of Cane Creek for many years. The first Brunswick stew at Cane Creek was made for the meeting's first Fall Festival in 1948. A large washpot over an open fire was used to hold the mixture of beef, chicken, pork, and various vegetables. On this particular occasion, a program had been planned for the morning, with Kerr Scott as the speaker. Because the stew required constant stirring, that task was assigned to two or three of the younger girls. Having been one of the girls, this writer can testify that we were delighted to assume the responsibility for stirring the stew because we escaped the confines of the planned program and what we thought would be a dull speech . What we did not know was that the so–called "dull speechmaker" would soon be the governor of North Carolina.

A washpot over an open fire that required constant stirring was the way to make Brunswick stew at Cane Creek until the late 1970s, when the pothouse was built. At that time, gas replaced wood as the fuel for cooking the stew. Unfortunately, the constant stirring is still required.

Turmoil in a Quaker Community

For many years life among the Quakers who had settled along Cane Creek was peaceful. Farmers tilled their fields; the blacksmith hammered at his forge; Simon Dixon kept his mill wheel turning; bonnetted women and black-hatted men went to meeting on First Day. This group of Friends prospered in the years following the establishment of Cane Creek Meeting. In other places, however, events were taking place that would shake the peaceful Quaker community and challenge its determination to remain "apart from things worldly."

In the eastern part of the colony at New Bern, Governor Tryon was building for himself an enormously expensive palace. Its cost (£15,000) would place an unbearable tax burden on the farmers who had settled in the Piedmont section of North Carolina.

In "Olde England," the Earl of Granville paid a gambling debt to Lord Burrington, a former governor of Carolina, with ten thousand acres of land in the colony. Deeding this same tract of land to Edward Mosely along with Granville's other acreage without separating the two tracts would add to the confusion in drawing up deeds in the future. Mosely served as Granville's land agent for several years until he was replaced in the early 1760s by two unscrupulous men, Childs and Corbin. It was at this point that corruption and greed began to enter into land deed transactions (Whitaker 21).

One of the agents — it is not clear which — tricked several settlers by pretending to be a lawyer. As such, he pronounced many of the farmers' deeds invalid because they were signed, "Granville, by his agent" rather than "The Right Honourable Granville, by his agent." As a result of this and other forms of trickery, some of the land was sold with an immense profit going to the land agent.

By 1766, the corruption had extended to the collection of taxes, which were already exorbitant. One couple was charged fifteen pounds — about $75.00 — for a wedding license (Stuart 2). If a farmer could not pay the excessive tax levied on his farm, he might find that his plow or his cow or his crop would be confiscated. Homes were invaded and any silverware, fine china, or precious hand-woven linen and woolen goods brought from the old country that could be found were taken despite the desperate and tearful protests of the grief-stricken housewives. It is said that on at least one occasion a farmer's wife had the dress taken from her back and sold to the highest bidder to pay the taxes on the farm. These tax collectors were generally accompanied by armed guards, and Governor Tryon himself admitted that "the Sheriffs have embezzled more than one-half the public money ordered to be raised and collected by them" (Whitaker 21).

Protest was in the air. Existing conditions gave rise to the Regulator Movement, which was an effort on the part of the tax-burdened farmers to "regulate" the affairs of the Colony in accordance with reasonable justice and harmony. For the most part, the men who formed the Regulator Movement were honest, honorable men who believed that the rampant injustices to which they were subjected could be corrected through "true and proper regulation."

It was during this period of unrest and protest throughout the Piedmont area, now known as Alamance, Chatham, and Guilford counties, that one of the most unusual members of Cane Creek entered the scene. Herman Husband was a convinced Quaker. His brother had led him to become a Friend in Maryland in 1724, and by 1751 he had migrated to eastern North Carolina. He joined Carver's Creek Meeting in Bladen County, and that meeting later granted him a certificate of removal to Cane Creek Meeting. The receipt of Husband's certificate was recorded in the Cane Creek Minutes of Twelfth month 1755.

Husband was apparently not satisfied with the local situation, as he left in 1759 for West River in Maryland (Weeks 179). Wanderlust seemed to afflict him, however, and he returned to Cane Creek in July 1761, this time taking possession of land along Sandy Creek. Something other than wanderlust may have facilitated his return because in less than a year he had married Mary Pugh, the daughter of one of his neighbors. In the Cane Creek Monthly Meeting Minutes, Seventh month 1762, "Friends reported that the marriage of Herman Husband and Mary Pugh had been accomplished orderly."

Husband was attracted to the cause of those who were being tricked and cheated by the government, and he helped organize the group of protesters who called themselves the Regulators. Governor Tryon, on the other hand, called them "a faction of Baptists and

Quakers trying to overcome the Church of England" (Weeks 178). Husband became the spokesman for the Regulators, and several times he petitioned the court and Governor Tryon for redress, asking that the colonists' grievances be heard. He also wrote and distributed pamphlets explaining the position of the Regulators. From accounts of Husband's life, we learn that he was quite outspoken and opinionated. This latter characteristic would get him into trouble with the Quakers.

A controversy began at Cane Creek that has become known through the years as the "Rachel Wright Affair." In his book, *Southern Quakers and Slavery*, Stephen B. Weeks explains it thusly: Rachel Wright, a "weighty Friend," committed some disorder. She was duly "complained of," and, to settle the matter according to Friends discipline, she offered a paper condemning her behavior, which was accepted. Then for some reason now unknown, she asked for a certificate to travel to Fredericksburg, Virginia. Some members of the monthly meeting did not want to give her the certificate, which would have functioned partly as a letter of introduction to other Friends and partly as an official endorsement by the meeting. A wrangle resulted and the meeting refused to grant the certificate. The matter was appealed to Western Quarterly Meeting, which advised that the certificate be granted (180).

Herman Husband, though, did not approve of the decision and in typical fashion was very vocal in his disapproval — so much so that, in January 1764, the meeting disowned him for "speaking against the actions and transactions of this meeting." As for Husband's reaction, there is an old story that when he heard about the disownment, he sat down, took off his shoes, shook the "dirt of Quakerism" off them, put them back on, and walked away.

However, the Wright affair was not over, and Husband's influence continued to be felt in the meeting. Some of his friends signed a paper expressing dissatisfaction with the meeting's decision to disown Husband. At this point the quarterly meeting offered the following advice (although it is unclear whether advice had been requested): "appoint a committee to deal with the malcontents' leaders." This group included Jos. Maddock, Isaac Vernon, Thomas Branson, John and William Marshall, Jonathan Cell, and "divers others." In February 1764, the committee reported that "there might be dangerous consequences to allow them [the malcontents] to be active members until suitable satisfaction is made for their outgoings." Maddock, Cell, and the Marshalls appealed the matter to the yearly meeting, which responded that Western Quarterly Meeting had done wrong in granting a certificate to Rachel Wright in the first place. Furthermore, the quarterly meeting should restore to active membership those who had signed papers expressing dissatisfaction with the disownment of Herman Husband. The quarterly meeting, accordingly, acknowledged itself wrong in the matter of Rachel Wright and restored the persons under the ban to active membership. Herman Husband's disownment, however, was not rescinded. (Griffin "History" 21).

There is no record of what happened to Husband's first wife, Mary Pugh, but his choice of a second wife, Amy Allen, again caused controversy within the meeting. This second marriage made him a brother-in-law of Simon Dixon, which would cause still more controversy in the next few years. A monthly meeting minute dated Fifth month 1765 reads, "Amy Allen Husband disowned for marrying out of unity." Eleven months later the Minutes reveal that three women and sixteen men were complained of for attending the marriage, which "was not accomplished according to the good order of Friends." Moreover, Amy's mother, Phoebe Allen Cox, was complained of for consenting to the marriage and accompanying her daughter. Once again the quarterly meeting and the yearly meeting were drawn into the local matter involving Husband.

Fifteen months after the wedding, Ninth month 1766, the

committee appointed to visit with those who were complained of reported that these persons were unwilling to condemn their conduct. The committee then asked that a "testification" be prepared against them. The papers were presented to those involved and the meeting disowned them.

In the meantime, Herman Husband had continued to support the cause of the Regulators, writing tracts denouncing unfair taxes and corrupt land dealings, and arranging meetings of the dissenters. The Colonial records show some aspects of the trouble, as well as the involvement of some of the members of Cane Creek with the Regulator movement. The following letter, dated May 10, 1768, from William Piggatt (Pickett) to Edmund Fanning, Governor Tryon's representative at Hillsborough, recalls some of the tension of the time:

Those that calls themselves Regulators has entertained an opinion that brother Jeremiah and I was Qualifyed when we were at court that Simon Dixon and Harmon Husbands was the Ringleaders of the mob and we understand that we are much threatened on the account of it therefore if thee would be pleased to send a few lines to Simon Dixon wheather it be true or foulse thee will oblege thy friend and well wishor (*Regulator Papers* 745–746).

Who threatened whom? It is not clear, but Fanning did indeed write to Simon Dixon as requested by Piggatt in May 1768:

I this day received the inclosed letter from Mr. William Piggatt and in answer thereto and in compliance with his request, I do, in Justice to the wrongfully blamed and accused, Hereby certify that I do not know neither do I believe, or did I ever hear that any information was ever made by the either of the said William or Jeremiah Piggatt on their solemn Information or otherwise against yourself

Harmon Husbands or any other person concerning their being engaged in the late miserable unhappy disturbance in this County (*Regulator Papers* 745–746).

However, Regulator advertisement number eight dated April 30, 1768 seems to show that Fanning had been misinformed.

At a general meeting of regulators on April 30th it was laid before us an appointment of the officers by the means of the Revd Mr micklejohn to meet us the 11th day of May next to settle the several matters of difference between us and it was agreed on that we will send 12 men that we have chosen to meet on the said 11th day of May at Thomas Lindley's when we hope things will be set in a fair way for an amicable settlement and Mr Hamilton is appointed to contrive them a copy hereof and bring from under our [their] hands if they will meet us.

The signers of this advertisement included three men from Cane Creek: Herman Husband, William Cox, and Simon Dixon (*Regulator Papers* 745–746).

Governor William Tryon arrived in Hillsborough on July 6, 1768 to stabilize the situation there. Previously, Governor Tryon had given James Hunter, one of the Regulators, a letter in which he gave his assurances of just treatment for the grievances claimed by the Regulators. Governor Tryon hoped that this would placate the Regulators, but he soon found this was not to be, for they continued holding their meetings. The matters reached a climax when, on August 10, 1768, a report was made to the Governor that

upward of 500 men had "rendezvoused" at Simon Dixons within twenty miles of the Town, with a firm resolution of coming into town the next day and to do mischief, and as a testimony of their intentions, they gave notice to some families immediately to carry their wives and children out of the town (*Regulator Papers* 127).

The mischief intended was to burn the town (Hillsborough) if their requests were not met. Fortunately, the insurgents were stopped when the leaders of the Regulators met with Tryon the next day. He assured them he would satisfy their demands.

As Herman Husband's popularity increased with the Regulators and their sympathizers, he was growing in disfavor with Governor Tryon and his representatives. The differences between the two groups continued to intensify, finally culminating in the Battle of Alamance on May 16, 1771, in which Herman Husband took no part. On the eve of the battle, he fled northward in disguise, toward Maryland.

There is a local story about Husband's journey north. As he traveled, dressed in homespun and riding an ancient swaybacked horse, he was approached by a group of soldiers who asked him if he had seen anything of a man riding fast along the trail. Husband assured them that he had not, and when they asked him where he was going, he replied that he was about his Father's business. The soldiers thought that he was a harmless old preacher and asked him to deliver a note for them in the next village. The note was addressed to Squire E____, a Tory, and read:

> Husband has escaped. He got word of our approach and barely saved himself. If he comes your way, have him taken. He must not escape.

The note was signed, "Corning." Husband carried it to the squire, who, after reading it, thanked him and, in gratitude for this service to the Tories, wrote him a permit allowing him to travel. After thanking the squire, Husband continued on his journey northward and, as far as is known, never returned to the Cane Creek area (Griffin Notes).

A week after the battle, on May 23, 1771, William Tryon ordered Captain Simon Bright "to go to Dixon's Mill, take possession of the same, and make a report to me of the quantity therein, and load 4 waggons [sic] with flour or corn whichever can be had." This order was apparently due to Tryon's belief that Simon Dixon supported the Regulators. Additionally, in a separate requisition the governor levied the Cane Creek settlement for forty–eight barrels of flour; making a note of the fact that sixty–three had been delivered. This would have amounted to about sixteen wagons of supplies for Tryon's army. However, it is not clear whether or not the entire amount was actually delivered. When Captain Bright and his men left Dixon's Mill with the four "waggons" of flour, the regulators intercepted them, but a short time later Tryon's men were able to recapture the supplies. Upon hearing about the adventure, Governor Tryon ordered his men to take three additional loads from Simon Dixon's Mill, "the owner having favored and assisted Rebels" (Regulator Papers).

The extent of the involvement with the Regulators by members of Cane Creek Meeting is not clear. No doubt there were some who supported and assisted the Regulators from the beginning. As early as 1766, seven members of the meeting had been disowned for attending a disorderly mass meeting (Griffin "History" 21). Could this have been a protest meeting of the Regulators? It seems possible, for Governor Tryon had just levied taxes for his new palace in New Bern at that time.

The matter of the flour was not over. The ever prudent Quakers petitioned the General Assembly of North Carolina on November 7, 1772, for payment for the flour.

From our monthly Meeting of the people called Quakers Held at Cain Creek in the County of Orange and Province of North Carolina the Seventh day of the Eleventh month 1772 —

To Josiah Martin Esqr. Governor and Commander in Chief in and over said province — and to the Councell, Speaker and members of the house of Assembly.

Do We as Humble dependents Earnestly Crave your Attention; and may these few lines seek Acceptance with You; that as we spread our Remonstrances before you; It may be your pleasure to have us redressed; for it is our Principle and known practice as a Society; to be subordinate and Peaceble under Government altho deviated from by some who make Profession as we do; for which the Severall Sheriffs can bear us record; that when their passing about in their respective Services was thought dangerous; that numbers of us Conveyed our money for our taxes; to the Severall Sheriffs Thereof; When come due and Payable, as being willing to exert our selves to the support of our Gracious King and Government; well knowing from whose clemency we as a people enjoy Great Priviledges —

Now the moving instance which we have to lay before you is that whereas Governor William Tryon; requested us to furnish him with Six Waggon Load of Flower; to gether with Six Waggons and Teams; in the campaign against the Regulators; which request we complyed with in exspectation of being paid for the same; and whereas we understand; there hath been but a small part at the last sitting of Assembly; therefore we humbly intrest You; to take it into Consideration; and grant this our petition for it otherwise the Burten thereof is most likely to fall on few in the discharge and settlement thereof; which may prove the means of Rendering some of us incapable of the punctuall of our other respective debts, therefore we Earnestly crave; that you condesind to Administer to our Releof [relief] and we ask with Humble hearts; being in duty bound, we shall return due Acknowledgements.

> Signed in and behalf of the said
> Meeting (*Regulator Papers*).

The petition was signed by Chris Huffey, Jeremiah Piggot, and twenty–two others. The quaint parlance of another era cannot hide the calculated purpose of the petition. First, they reminded the Governor and the Assembly of their patriotism and loyalty to the Crown; then they asked for redress, and finally, almost threatened not to continue to pay their taxes. Clever as it may have been, the gambit did not work, for no money was forthcoming from the Assembly.

The price of six loads of flour (flower) would forever remain unpaid. However, it has added spice to the tales of the Regulators that have passed from one generation to the next.

THE REVOLUTIONARY WAR

S ome historians have called the Battle of
Alamance the opening battle of the Revolutionary War. William Powell, in *The War of
the Revolution and the Battle of Alamance*, says the
real significance of the battle "lies in the fact that it
stood as a grand object lesson to the people of the
whole country. It set them to thinking of armed
resistance and showed them how weak might be the
British effort to surpass a full–scale revolution"
(28).

No doubt many Quakers found themselves at
odds with their neighbors over the rising tumult
which would erupt in less than five years into full–
fledged war caused by changes in attitudes toward
the government.

Just as the Minutes of Cane Creek Monthly Meeting contain no reference to the Regulator movement other than through disownments, there is no mention of the Revolutionary War. Instead, there is a record of a peaceable people trying to maintain an orderly and God–fearing way of life in the midst of what were turbulent times. No doubt they tried to live as best they could according to their Declaration of Faith: "We feel bound explicitly to avow our unshaken persuasion that all war is utterly incompatible with the plain precepts of our divine Lord and Law–giver" (*Faith and Practice* 28).

To the Quakers, "taxation without representation" did not mean taxes levied by George III on tea or stamps, but rather the portion of their taxes that went to support the Church of England. In April 1767, according to the Minutes, Levi Branson and William Piggot brought a concern to monthly meeting, requesting the right "to inspect what part of our tax is for the support of the 'hireling priest'." They were allowed to inspect the Vestries Book. In all probability, this book was at Hillsborough, the seat of the local government. If so, a journey of some twenty miles was necessary. Most men willing to travel that distance would have been concerned about a personal tax rather than a tax involving religion. Most men would have been appalled to find after such a journey that the tax amounted to one shilling and one farthing "as near as we can come at." How like the Quakers to be primarily concerned about religious matters in a society threatening to erupt at any time.

Since the beginning of the war in 1776, most of the battles had been fought in the Northern Colonies. But by 1781, the war had reached the South. Lord Cornwallis, commander of the British forces in the South, had engaged General Nathanael Greene at Guilford Court House. On the second day after the battle, Cornwallis began his march toward Wilmington. His planned campsites would be near grist mills along the route. His army was traveling without supply wagons and it would be necessary to forage off the countryside. His first encampment was at Bell's Mill in Randolph County. From there he intended to go to Ramsey's Mill, near Moncure in Chatham County. However, for some reason known only to Cornwallis, he did not take the most direct route to Ramsey's. He, instead, turned aside and stopped at Simon Dixon's Mill (Dixon 1).

The British made camp north of the mill in a grain field. Cornwallis chose for his headquarters Simon Dixon's stone house which stood quite nearby. The Dixon family was told to leave and not come back until the army had moved on.

Simon Dixon had been warned of the approach of the British soldiers. He had chosen to leave the area and stay with a friend named Mebane near the Hawfields community. Simon was fearful that his reputed involvement with the Regulator movement might endanger his life at the hands of the British.

The soldiers stacked their guns in two long rows between the mill and the Dixon house. The hillside was dotted with camp fires as the men rested. The smell of roasting meat filled the air. According to private records, the soldiers killed 250 sheep, fifty cows, and scoured the neighborhood for bee hives until they had about eighty. The cattle were butchered near the meetinghouse. The benches, which were single board seats with no backs, were carried into the yard and used as "butcher tables." The benches continued to be used in the meetinghouse, still bearing axe marks and blood stains until a fire in 1879 destroyed them.

Cornwallis spent most of his time resting in a large armchair by the fire inside the house. Perhaps he was reliving the battle, which to his military mind had been a loss. Perhaps he was planning strategy as he contemplated the fire. Some of the soldiers tried to use the mill but found the grinding stones had been jammed together. Simon Dixon had thwarted the Tories' attempts to use his mill and to find his gold. After a week of rest, the army left the community and continued on its way to Wilmington.

Destruction and devastation could be seen throughout the community, but some things had not changed. The meetinghouse still stood, even though its benches bore the butcher's axe marks. The Dixon mill and home were still there, and the mill would continue to serve the community for many years. The rock wall, reminiscent of a Pennsylvania heritage, still marked the road to the meetinghouse. The marks and ravages left by the British army would soon pass away, but the memory of their visit would remain. A more permanent reminder of their stay in the community was the newly made graves for six British soldiers who died during the encampment and were buried in the cemetery. Their names, however, have long been forgotten.

Dixon's Mill at Snow Camp

From time to time, relics from that long ago time surface and the residents of the community are reminded quite vividly of their ancestors' brush with history. Around 1920, some young boys found a cannon ball in the rock wall while walking along the top of it — a favorite pastime in years gone by. Also in the 1920s, gravediggers unearthed some mini–balls in the cemetery. No one will ever know how these and other artifacts came to be where they were found. However, discoveries such as these revive the folklore that perhaps Cornwallis had buried cannon as well as some of his soldiers in the meetinghouse cemetery.

It seems that, according to British war records, Cornwallis captured two of Nathanael Greene's cannon. Tradition says that the English pulled them as far as Cane Creek. However, they slowed the army and became a liability. Eyewitnesses told of seeing the cannon when the British arrived, but they did not see them when the British left. This tale has been passed from generation to generation. Burial of the cannon seemed a likely solution that would prevent recapture. Some believe that the cannon were submerged in the Cane Creek east of Dixon's Mill. Perhaps, some time in the future, someone will discover their hiding place if there is one.

Also, folklore indicates that Cornwallis gave the settlement its name of Snow Camp, providing a second explanation for this name. Supposedly, snow fell while the British army was encamped at Cane Creek. However, as the fourth week in March is rather late for snow in this area, it seems unlikely that this happened.

The Dixon family returned to their home shortly after the departure of their "guests." In a few days, Simon was taken ill with some kind of camp fever and died. Local tradition suggests that Simon Dixon was tortured by Cornwallis and his men. While this cannot be fully substantiated, it is true that Dixon died shortly thereafter.

The long–range effects of the Revolutionary War continued into the nineteenth century. Some families chose to migrate rather than face the difficulties of the postwar era. Thus, a pattern was established which would continue for the next fifty years.

Prior to the war some Friends had moved south to be united with Quaker settlements in South Carolina: Bush River, Cane Creek, Fredricksburg (later Wateree), and Wrightsborough in Georgia (Griffin "History" 25). However, by the late 1700s the southern settlements did not seem as attractive as they once had been. After the Revolutionary War was over, land in eastern Tennessee became available to settlers. Grants of land there were given to those who applied in return for services they had rendered in the cause for independence. While Friends did not actually participate in the war, many joined their friends and neighbors in the westward migration. Active meetings were begun in the new settlements: Lost Creek, Newberry, Friendsville, and New Hope. Between 1795 and 1804, twelve certificates to Lost Creek and New Hope were granted (Weeks 265).

Then in the early 1800s, the lure of the West began to attract families. The land in the Carolinas was becoming poorer each year and little was known about soil improvement. Land in the West was rich and cheap. In 1804 the first parties went to Ohio. In that year, the Minutes indicate five certificates of removal to Miami, Ohio. The total number of families who migrated to Ohio between the years 1801 and 1810 was forty–three (Weeks 269).

SLAVERY

Query six was read from the Discipline in a session of Cane Creek Monthly Meeting First month 1784:

Are Friends clear of importing, purchasing, disposing of or holding mankind as slave, and do they use those well who are under their care, through management or otherwise endeavoring to encourage them in a virtuous life?

The scourge of slavery spread across the land as the slave trade flourished. Plantation owners and farmers alike recognized the economic advantage that slave labor provided. However, there were those who opposed the enslavement of human beings, believing instead that slavery did not correspond with the teachings of Jesus Christ. John Woolman, often referred to as the "Quaker Conscience," undertook the enlightenment of his fellow Quakers regarding the evils of slavery. He visited the Carolinas for the second time in 1757. During this visit he wrote Friends at New Garden and Cane Creek:

> And now dear friends and brethren as you are improving a wilderness, and may be numbered amongst the first planters in one part of the province, I Beseech you wisely to consider the force of your examples, and think how much your successors may be thereby affected. It is a help in a country, yea, a great favor, when customs first settled are agreeable to sound wisdom (*Journal* 65).

North Carolina Yearly Meeting expressed grave concern over the practice of its members' holding slaves as property. Near the beginning of the nineteenth century, the yearly meeting itself accepted the ownership of slaves and placed them under its care. This practice ensured that these persons who would have had no legal status as freed men would be treated fairly. They would be paid wages for their labor and would not be separated from their families. These people came to be known as Quaker Free Negroes.

An extract from a yearly meeting epistle was read in the monthly meeting for business Eleventh month 1800. Cane Creek was asked to appoint a committee to "unite with a Quarterly Meeting Committee in inspecting into the circumstances of the black people amongst Friends and in doing what may appear expedient in their power for the enlargement of them and also in labouring with instruction and usage of those blacks that are under their care." No committee names are recorded, so it not clear if Cane Creek Meeting complied with the request.

In 1809 the yearly meeting asked for "the general mind of how to act in the future in the cases of holding slaves." This time Cane Creek replied (Fourth month 1810): "It is agreed that the authority of the agents appointed by the yearly meeting be suspended or entirely cease, and that no more people of color be received in that way by the yearly meeting."

There were few slave owners, Quaker or otherwise, in the Snow Camp area. The farms were small, the families usually large, and owning slaves was not economically feasible. These practicalities only bolstered the people's sense of injustice against the practice of owning slaves.

A few Friends did, however, have slaves. When this occurred, the meeting took action. According to the Minutes of November 1798, Marshall and David Vestal were asked to visit a father and son who were involved in "purchasing and holding negroes." They were "to convince their minds of the inconsistence of such conduct." Readers of this directive can only wonder if the meeting thought it would be easier to convince minds rather than persuade consciences. One woman was disowned for holding and selling slaves in 1846.

Cane Creek Meeting may have been located in a rather remote area, removed from much of the political maneuvering of that era. They were not, however, removed from the seriousness of the slavery issue. In June 1823, the monthly meeting agreed to assist in removing "people of color" to Indiana, Ohio, and Illinois. A year later, in July 1824, they considered sending people of color to Haiti or wherever they chose to go. The meeting would help defray the cost of such endeavors.

The remoteness of Cane Creek served its members well in their decision to help the slaves. A station of the Underground Railroad was located one and one–half miles south of the meetinghouse. The

Underground Railroad was a means of helping slaves escape from their masters and flee North to freedom. Many Quakers in North Carolina were involved in this work. The Underground Railroad was a network of safe houses, called stations, across the state. The stations were located approximately one day's journey apart. Slaves who were escaping from their owners were guided from station to station, where they were hidden and cared for by the local citizens who defied the law and risked stiff penalties if caught. The paths between stations were marked with carefully hidden signs. For example, nails would be driven on a tree in a certain pattern indicating which fork of the trail should be taken. Another pattern might indicate that the farms close by had dogs.

At the station near Cane Creek, the slaves were housed in the home of William Kirkman. He had a two-story log house, the upstairs of which was large enough for the slaves to use as a dining room and also a sleeping room when there was no immediate threat from their pursuers. The Kirkmans were assisted by members of Cane Creek and possibly other churches in the area with donations of food, bedding, clothing, and other items the slaves might need. Since the slaves had nothing except their clothing with them, these supplies had to be replenished each time the station was used. During the day the slaves hid in a large hollow log located some distance from the house. Only when it was dark and deemed to be safe would they dare venture into the house to eat and rest. The slaves were tutored in ways to survive as they made their way to freedom in the North. Something as simple as gathering tomatoes from a farmhouse garden patch might give their hunters a clue about their presence. They were told never to pick all the tomatoes from one vine but rather to pick one tomato from several vines creating a less noticeable loss (Finley Coble Interview).

The Kirkman property is today part of the farm of Finley and Georgia Coble. Nothing remains of the house. Only a large rock in front of their barn bears silent testimony to the desperate men and women who passed by it on their way to freedom and also to the courageous Quaker men and women who helped them.

In the decade just prior to the Civil War, some members of Cane Creek Meeting became involved in a more public antislavery movement. They learned that some of their neighbors to the south on the edge of Chatham County had been left without a church home when their denomination, the Methodist Episcopal Church, had split over the slavery issue. The split led to the formation of a new denomination, the Wesleyan Methodist Connection of America. When the news of this new denomination reached the Cane Creek community, it seemed to be the perfect vehicle for the families without a church and their sympathetic neighbors in Cane Creek to exercise their antislavery beliefs. Consequently, both groups collaborated on a request to the Wesleyan organization for a preacher. The arrival of the Rev. Adam Crooks in October 1847, initiated an evangelistic and church organizing ministry which resulted in the construction of a new church in the Cane Creek community.

The building for this new church was built on land deeded to the trustees by Simon Dixon, a descendant of the early settler by that name. The trustees were George Councilman, Micajah McPherson, and Alfred Vestal. The original deed signed by Simon Dixon was witnessed by Hugh Dixon and Margaret Williams. William Thompson and his wife were also strong supporters of the new ministry in the area. The church was named Freedom's Hill (Nicholson 1).

This name seems appropriate since the building stood only a few yards from the Kirkman house. Even though the church had strong support from its Quaker neighbors, there were others in the area who did not like its antislavery stand and took strong measures to negate its appeal. Bullet holes in the siding of the building are

Freedom's Hill Wesleyan Methodist Church, built 1848

Interior of Freedom's Hill Church

evidence of the vehement emotions of the times. On several occasions, protesters fired into the building in an attempt to stop the worship services that were going on.

Over the years the church fell into disrepair as members died or moved away and interest waned. Finally, in the 1950s, the old building was moved to the Wesleyan Campground near Colfax, North Carolina.

There is no doubt that Cane Creek Meeting stood firmly against slavery. Surely during First day worship, voices spoke against the evil practice as "the Spirit gave them liberty to do so."

THE CIVIL WAR

T rue to Quaker tradition, very little was written about the Civil War in the Minutes of Cane Creek Meeting. Nevertheless, try as they would, their lives could not have escaped the events of the 1860s. Once again young men of the meeting would have to decide if they should join the army or remain true to their Quaker Peace Testimony. Their decision may have been made more difficult because there was a training camp at Company Shops, near Burlington, just a few miles away. Even though they might have known about the enlistment of friends and neighbors, it is unlikely they felt the pressure to enlist that their ancestors had felt during the Revolutionary

War. This war was different from the others in at least one respect. To some it had seemed a noble cause to fight for independence in 1776, but there would be nothing noble in fighting to preserve a culture that depended on slavery for its existence.

Alamance County saw little of the war itself. No major battles were fought nearby. The only soldiers to be seen were an occasional army patrol riding through looking for deserters, or sometimes the quartermasters' wagons looking for supplies. Other times it would be the conscription wagons looking for draftees and recruits.

The writer remembers her father telling the story of his grandfather, Isaac Holt Thompson, as it was told to him by his grandmother, Mary Ann Thompson. She had stood in the middle of the road surrounded by her small children and watched as the conscription wagon carried her husband to war. She remembered his face peering out of the back of the wagon as it carried him out of sight down the dusty road. She and the children had stood and watched the empty road long after the wagon had disappeared as if in so doing they could will it to come back. Mary Ann and the children would never see him again; he died on a Pennsylvania battlefield. Similar stories would be repeated over and over throughout the area.

The hardships suffered by the rest of the population were so intense and so devastating that Cane Creek Quakers could not have escaped them. While the violence of war did not reach the countryside around Cane Creek, violence of another kind erupted at the Freedom's Hill Church which, as previously stated, was located nearby. Confederate sympathizers aroused by the abolitionist stand of the church abducted Micajah McPherson, a leader and trustee of the Freedom's Hill Church, from his home and attempted to hang him. His wife and his grandson, Monroe Roach, watched as his abductors put a noose around his neck, tied him to a small dogwood tree and pushed him over a cliff. When they believed him to be

Micajah McPherson, a layman with convictions

dead, they cut him down and left him for dead. One account says his abductors made the remark as they removed the noose that they had another hanging to attend and needed the noose. Micajah McPherson cheated his abductors; he was still alive and remained so for some thirty years after the incident (Haines 3).

At a meeting held Ninth month 1863, a letter was read in monthly meeting from a called Meeting for Sufferings at Springfield Meeting in High Point. The letter protested the demands of the Confederate Government that one–tenth of the land's produce should be given to the government. It was the judgment of the Meeting for Sufferings that the tithe not be paid. It was felt that such payments and gifts only aided and prolonged the war. Reticent as ever, the clerk of Cane Creek Meeting did not record what decision, if any, was made by the monthly meeting.

Earlier in February of the same year, 1863, Milton Woody reported to the monthly meeting that he had "availed himself of the Exemption Act of The Confederate Congress." He offered to resign as clerk of the meeting, but his resignation was not accepted. Woody explained his actions in a letter to the monthly meeting. He was subject to conscription and had been forcibly taken into the Confederate Army. A uniform and equipment was given to him but he refused to accept them. He saw firsthand the "evils of the army." Woody felt he had no other choice but to pay the five–hundred dollar exemption fee and return home. This must have been, to him, the lesser of two evils.

Another man decided to pay the five hundred dollars for a replacement to take his place in the army. Ironically, the man who went into the army in his place was a member of Cane Creek but was not disowned by the meeting for joining the army. However, the man who paid him was disowned.

The migration to the West that had begun following the Revolutionary War had continued during the pre–Civil War period. Friends found the Indiana Territory very attractive. Between 1811 and 1820 thirty–one families migrated to Indiana. The next decade produced the most migration. Forty–seven certificates of removal were recorded during that time period. From 1831 to 1840, there were twenty–three (Weeks 269).

Certainly, one of the contributing factors to the large number of migrations during this period was the slavery issue. Friends who did not own slaves found it hard to compete economically with farmers who did. Also, there was a sense of impending crisis over the matter. As the war clouds had appeared on the horizon, several young men had made their way to Ohio or to Indiana to escape recruitment into the army.

The list of certificates of removal is quite long. Familiar names found on the list are Edwards, Hobson, Stout, Doan, Cox, Carter,

Harvey, Newlin, Hadley, Dixon, Moon, Marshall, Allen, Hackett, Wheeler, Hinshaw, Wells, and Pike.

The numbers alone are staggering, especially when one realizes that the numbers are for heads of families only. It is truly an understatement that the membership of Cane Creek Meeting was greatly depleted. Fortunately enough people remained for Cane Creek Meeting to continue. When peace was once again established, the Quakers began picking up the pieces of their lives and helping others do likewise.

Meetings for Worship and Business

The Quaker meeting for worship was, and still is, a vital part of the Quaker way of life. Before a meetinghouse could be built, early settlers held their worship services in their homes. Sometimes only the family would be present. At other times there would be two or three families gathered together. In either situation, the service would be a time of waiting, listening, and praying. The term "centering down" was used to explain the preliminary period of settling into the worship experience — a time when children were hushed, eyes were closed, and heads were bowed. In this way all the distractions which might come from the physical surroundings were minimized as much as possible.

At first there were no preachers or pastors as we have today. Instead there were "recorded ministers," which is a Quaker term designating those men and women who were recognized as having a "gift of ministry." They were the leaders of the meeting. One of their responsibilities was to be in charge of the worship services. As such they were said "to sit at the head of the meeting." During the worship service they would sit on the facing bench at the front of the meeting.

There were two worship services held each week: one on First day (Sunday) and the other on Fifth day (Thursday). Picture the scene: the men are on one side of the meeting room and the women on the other. At the front on the facing bench are the elders for this particular meeting. There is silence. After a while some one might rise and speak about something which he feels "has been laid on his heart." There might be others to rise and speak. Sometimes there would be no spoken word for the entire time. When those at the head of the meeting felt that the time had come to close the worship service, they would shake hands with each other. The other worshipers would shake hands also and the meeting was over.

It was the custom for both men and women to wear their hats and bonnets during the service. When a woman wished to speak in the meeting she would remove her bonnet, lay it on the lap of the woman sitting next to her, then rise and speak. The men removed their black broad–brimmed hats also before speaking. All men removed their hats during spoken prayer (Stuart 2).

Attendance at the weekly worship services was expected of all members. Most of the time this obligation was accepted willingly. The monthly meeting would inquire and deal with anyone who missed the services without a good reason to do so.

It is rather odd to think that regular worship service attendance could be amusing, but it certainly was on at least one occasion. Thomas Dixon was a faithful lifelong member of Cane Creek. He was a recorded minister and leader and as such often sat at the head of the meeting. One time Thomas Dixon was sick and could not attend the Fifth day service. When the time came to leave for the service the family dog began to bark in the front yard. When it became apparent to the dog that the family was not going to be leaving the farm on that particular afternoon, the dog ran to the meetinghouse, walked down the aisle to the bench where Thomas Dixon usually sat, and lay down under the bench. The dog lay quietly for about an hour, then got up, walked out and went home.

The practice of speaking during the worship service has caused some rather amusing things to happen, also. One afternoon during the Fifth day services, there were a number of people who spoke on a variety of subjects. A little boy sat quietly listening as one after another rose to speak. Finally, he decided that it was his turn. He stood, removed his hat and said, "When I came by the mill, the big wheel was going round and round."

The practice of waiting quietly and allowing time for Friends to share in the meeting has not always been understood by visitors. One young man accompanied his girl friend to meeting. As one person after another spoke during the open worship he became more and more agitated. As it happened the people who were speaking in the meeting seemed to him to be rising in some pattern which had begun with a person near the front and moved nearer and nearer the back of the meeting room. The young man became terrified when it appeared to him that he was going to be next in line to speak. He was just about ready to bolt for the door when the meeting was concluded.

Today, the worship services at Cane Creek are very different from the early meetings for worship. However, Friends continue to worship together and share as the Lord leads them. Periods of silent meditation and open worship remain important elements of each service.

Cane Creek members, ca. 1947. J. Waldo Woody, pastor.

While music is an integral part of worship at Cane Creek Meeting today, early Friends did not approve of singing or of the use of musical instruments, either in worship services or in the home. As late as 1830, one member was disowned at Cane Creek for attending a singing school in the community.

Singing schools were quite the rage in the latter part of the

86

1800s and into the first quarter of the twentieth century. Participants were taught to read the music, not by the place of the note on space or line of the staff but by the shape of the notes. A certain shape, such as a diamond, a triangle, a square, or a rectangle, stood for a certain note and by memorizing the shapes, one could be taught to sound the note needed for the song. Churches within the community banded together to hire the teacher for the school which usually lasted a week or possibly two. Such schools were well attended for not only did they offer music instruction, they also provided a social occasion for visiting neighbors.

It is not known when congregational singing began or when an organized choir was begun at Cane Creek. The first musical instrument used was a small folding organ. It was kept at the home of Eula and Florence Dixon just across the road from the meetinghouse. On First day someone would bring it to the meetinghouse where it was played at the beginning and the closing of Sunday School. During the worship service it was folded and stored under a bench. The older members of the meeting were quite opposed to the use of the organ. It must have taken some time for its use to become generally accepted (Stuart 4).

In 1915 Hayes Thompson gave the first large reed organ to the meeting. In 1920 Callie Green collected donations for a piano (Griffin Notes). The reed organ was destroyed in the fire of 1942 and was not replaced. Only piano music was used until the early 1950s when an electric organ was purchased.

Unlike Friends of long ago who protested the use of music in the meeting, present day Friends at Cane Creek would protest if there were no music on Sunday mornings during worship. Music has become an important and vital part of the life of the meeting.

So central was worship in the life of early Friends that necessary business items were handled in a meeting for worship in which business was transacted. The primary objective was to ascertain that which was right and to discern God's will. No votes were taken, for Friends did not feel that this was in accord with their seeking–worship process.

The presiding clerk's job then as now was to determine the "mind of the meeting." Should the clerk determine there was not unity and agreement among members, the matter under consideration would be postponed until another time. It might be necessary for the clerk to make several postponements. Decisions made in this manner negated the possibility of much dissension and hard feelings between members, thus freeing them to live a more purposeful life.

The monthly meeting Minutes for the early years were quite sparse. Quite often it was recorded that various reports were made, with no indication of the contents. The quarterly meeting required a written answer to queries concerning the spiritual life of the

Jesse Thompson, trustee, Sunday school superintendent and teacher, and his wife, Annie Andrews Thompson.

meeting. The monthly meeting did not neglect this responsibility; neither did they record their answers. One is left wondering. Fortunately, statistical reports were recorded from time to time.

A comparison of the report for 1881 with that of 1981, one hundred years later, may prove interesting; note the differences. Our present day report seems to be largely concerned with finances, while no mention was made of money in 1881. (See Appendix.)

Cane Creek Monthly Meeting was organized according to the tradition of Friends. There were separate business meetings for men and women. The early meetinghouses were designed for this purpose. A long row of shutters ran the length of the meeting room and these could be opened during worship but closed for the business sessions. Business matters originating in either the men's or women's side were usually not settled until both meetings were consulted.

The practice of holding two business meetings was discontinued at Cane Creek in 1877. According to the Minutes, the last such meeting was held Twelfth month 1877. This predated the yearly meeting's discontinuation of separate meetings by some twenty years.

For more than a hundred years, marriages among Friends were under the care of the monthly meeting. The couple would state their intentions and ask for the approval of the meeting. A clearness committee would be appointed to investigate the situation. If no hindrances were found and the couple seemed to be "clear" in every way, the committee would so inform the monthly meeting and the wedding would proceed. However, the monthly meeting selected the date and time for the marriage and appointed a committee to attend the wedding to see that it was conducted in a proper and "seemly" manner. One might think this would be the end of the monthly meeting's involvement but not so, for there was one more committee report to be made. The monthly meeting expected a report about the wedding and any festivities after the ceremony. Scattered throughout the Cane Creek Minutes, one can read where a marriage was conducted in a seemly fashion or in other cases, there was evidence of unseemly and frivolous entertainment.

The ceremony itself would be in an appointed meeting for worship. At the appropriate time, usually after a period of open worship, the couple stood and spoke their vows to each other, with no minister officiating. The elders of the meeting were in charge. A rather lengthy certificate was signed by the groom and bride first, and then by those present and the marriage would be recorded in the Minutes of the meeting.

Ed and Lorraine Griffin were the last couple to be married after the manner of Friends at Cane Creek Meeting. Their marriage occurred on June 28, 1916 (Stuart 4).

One of the more interesting and unusual committees that has been active in the life of the monthly meeting dates from the first decade of the 1900s. It was the Transportation and Entertainment Committee. Then, as now, Cane Creek was some distance from the train station. The job of this committee was to meet the trains and transport visitors to and from the meeting. Also, they were to see that places were provided for their hospitality while in the community. The committee, as listed in the Minutes of June 1909, consisted of Hayes Thompson, Lyndon Stuart, Dougan Thompson, Flora Stout, Sarah Pickett, Cicero Stuart, Harrison Thompson, and Mary J. Coble. Unfortunately, there is no record of the method of transportation. Most likely, it would have been by horse and buggy. Pity the poor travelers who, after a long and tiring train trip, would be subjected to at least a two–hour buggy ride before arriving at their destination.

A good example of the necessity for a transportation committee may be seen in the following diary account of the travels of Mary

Cane Creek women, early 1900s. Left to right: Ella Thompson, Sybil Thompson, Martha Thompson, Eliza Johnson, and Mary Coble.

C. Woody, a recorded Friends minister, who was traveling for the Evangelism and Church Extension Committee of the yearly meeting in February 1900. Mary Edith Hinshaw recounts the trip in her book, *Pioneers in Quaker Education*:

> Friday, February 9: Off for Liberty (on the Train). Reached Cane Creek Quarterly Meeting at 4. Glorious meeting of ministry and oversight. Didn't close until 5 p.m.

Saturday: Rain, sleet. Meeting at 11. Good Crowd — good meeting — held until 3:30. Business passed so easily — scarcely knew it. Discipline. Close preaching. Many quit tobacco.

Sunday, 11: Sleet. Icicles everywhere., every limb fringed. Sunday School, Glorious meeting — 2 sessions in all.

The account further states that "Mary stayed at Zeno Dixon's home next door to Cane Creek Meetinghouse. She reported a chilly buggy ride to Nathaniel Woody's at Saxapahaw on Sunday night (9 miles in $1^1/_2$ hours. Quick Time)" (85).

One cannot read of such an endeavor without renewed admiration and appreciation for the dedication of those whose legacy we enjoy today.

THE SPOKEN MINISTRY

Quakers are well known for their quietness and for the silences in their worship services. Quakers also believe that the spoken or vocal ministry is equally important and vital to the meeting. Friends have long recognized that some members were able to minister to others through the spoken word. Members of the meeting who seemed to exercise this particular talent were recognized by the meeting as "having a gift of ministry." This talent would be duly noted in the Minutes of the meeting. The individual would then be considered a "recorded minister in the Society of Friends." In more recent years it has become necessary to have the quarterly meeting and the yearly meeting give approval to the recording process.

York Teague, resident pastor and worker.

Abigail Pike, Joseph Cloud, and Hannah Cloud were among the first persons to be recorded as ministers at Cane Creek. Through the years others also have been recorded. The list includes Harrison Allen, Jasper Thompson, Thomas Dixon, Maurice Stuart, Walter Allen, Milo Dixon, Zeno Dixon, Roxie Dixon White, York Teague, Blake Wright, Luther Mc-Pherson, Paula Teague, and Brian Wilson.

Charity Wright Cook, Eliza Armstrong Cox, William Dixon, Amy Thompson, and Lindley Moore were also recorded ministers. Although their ministries were in other states, their roots were in the Cane Creek Meeting.

The idea of a pastoral ministry began in the late 1800s. During this period, Thomas C. Hodgin held a revival at Cane Creek. He emphasized the need for pastoral service, and Friends' attitudes began to change. Thomas Hodgin continued to preach once or twice a month on First day for some time. It began to seem prudent for the meeting to consider some type of pastoral arrangements (Griffin "History" 40).

Pastoral Committee records indicate that the pastoral ministry began at Cane Creek in 1909 with Miles and Georgia Reece as ministers. They served until 1914. Rufus Pegg, Thomas Dixon, and Margaret Hackney were the ministers until Oscar and Belle Cox began their ministry in 1918 (Griffin "History" 41).

Local members who gave their services to the meeting were Milo Dixon, Maurice Stuart, and Thomas Dixon. Robert H. Melvin and Thomas Hendricks were part–time workers. Georgia Reece and Virgil Pike taught at Sylvan School and preached at Cane Creek on Sunday. There was no hired minister until 1918. At that time Oscar Cox and Edward Harris were employed to preach once each month for $50 a year.

In 1926 Walter Allen, a former member, returned from Kansas and served as pastor until his death in 1929. Elbert Newlin, then a student at Guilford College, took his place.

The practice of having a part–time minister continued until 1941, at which time Elbert Newlin returned to Cane Creek Meeting to become the first full–time pastor. He was paid $100

Lewis and Pearl McFarland, pastors at Cane Creek, 1932–36; superintendent of evangelism in North Carolina. Yearly Meeting, 1915–30.

a month, plus $13.50 a month for house rent.

The meeting soon recognized the fact that a full–time pastor and his family required a parsonage. Prior to this time, the ministers had lived in rented houses in the community. In March 1945, a fund to build a home for the minister and his family was started. Plans for construction were given a boost with the gift of one acre of land from Pearl Griffin. The land located on the Snow Camp–Siler City Road, near Thompson's Garage, proved to be a satisfactory building site. The modern, five–room, brick home was completed in 1947. The first ministers to live in the new parsonage were J. Waldo and Lutie Woody. The upstairs part of the house was finished in the early 1950s. This house would be home to all the ministers through 1990.

In the early summer of 1990, a new parsonage was constructed on an acre of land which had been donated to the meeting by David

Elbert and Inez Newlin, first full–time pastors at Cane Creek, 1941–45.

J. Waldo and Lutie Woody, pastors at Cane Creek, 1945–49.

Carter in memory of his mother, Kathryn Dixon Carter, wife of Norman Carter, a Friends minister. As in the past, this building was debt–free when the pastor, Dale Matthews, and his family moved in.

The pastoral ministers who have served Cane Creek Meeting are listed in the Appendix.

Religious Instruction

Friends believe that "In the providence of God, man has been entrusted with the responsibility of participating in his own creation. This is [sic], he has been given the capacity to grow, to become. He can assist in or thwart this mental and spiritual development" (*What Do Friends Believe?* 15). Therefore, religious instruction was an important part of the training of youth. It was considered the responsibility of the meeting as well as of the home.

The monthly meeting often reminded parents of their responsibility for their children. Surveys were conducted by the monthly meeting to ascertain the number who held devotions in the home. Those who did not were encouraged to do so.

Surveys also were made to find how many did not have Bibles in their homes. In 1833, it was reported that there were nine families without a Bible.

In 1848, twenty-seven Bibles were received from the Philadelphia Meeting and distributed to those who needed them. In February 1852, a committee of John Dixon and Miles Hobson gave this report of Bibles sold: "7 large $1.75 each; 8 small $.75 each; 1 damaged $.50; 2 were given to those who did not have copies; 7 large testaments sold at $.30 each (gave away one); 8 small leather bound at 12$^{1}/_{2}$ cents; 9 small muslin bound at 10 cents."

Friends have always felt the First Day Schools were of primary importance. Cane Creek was no exception. A committee was appointed to consider the subject of First Day Schools Third month 1752. What action resulted from this is not known. Apparently, First Day Schools were held for short periods of time throughout the first century of Cane Creek's existence. For example, in the Minutes of January 1858, it was recorded that "notice was given that First Day Scripture Schools were to be held throughout the summer in each of the Preparative Meetings."

One of the first acts of business following the close of the Civil War was the appointment of J. Milton Woody, Obed Marshburn, Alfred Cox, Calvin Thompson, W. T. Pickett, Caleb Dixon, and Bob Allen in April 1865, to use their "endeavors" to have a First Day School opened and carried on in each of the Preparative Meetings. Four months later in April 1865, Obed Marshburn reported that two schools had been held and one was still in operation. The first had fifty-four in attendance, with twenty-four members and thirty non-members. The second school had forty-eight pupils, thirty-two of whom were members.

A booklet, *The Little Visitor*, published by Sylvan Academy in 1868, states, "The Sabbath School at Cane Creek Church opened for the present year on Sunday 18th of October" (*Sylvanian* 9).

In March 1869, the monthly meeting appointed a committee to establish First Day Schools. Bible classes and other means of scriptural instruction were to be used. In October of that same year, the record indicates that the matter had been given some attention, for a school had operated in the Preparative Meetings through September.

Sabbath Schools or First Day Schools have been held with regularity since the latter part of the 1800s. From the Cane Creek Minutes for March 1880, one reads that the Cane Creek Sabbath School opened in the new house for the first time. William Long gave two medals to be awarded twelve months "hence" for the best behaved boy and girl in the Sabbath School.

Bible verses were taught to each class and then repeated to the congregation when the classes assembled in the meeting room for the closing exercises. One little girl did a little paraphrasing when she stood and repeated as her verse, "Thou shall not steal a house."

For many years Ruth M. Hinshaw gave illustrated blackboard lessons. She was a talented artist and made her subjects come "alive" as she illustrated the lesson for the day.

There have been many dedicated teachers in the First Day Schools, later called Sunday Schools, at Cane Creek. The beginners class was taught by three generations of the same family. Lydia Dixon began the tradition, to be followed by her daughter, Clara Pike, who was succeeded by her daughter, Anna Lois Dixon.

One of Anna Lois's favorite stories about her teaching experience involves a very rowdy youngster and the power of prayer. Anna Lois had a lot of trouble managing one little fellow. He would not sit still and climbed and jumped about the classroom every Sunday. Despite all her efforts, she had not been very successful in calming him. One Sunday was particularly bad. Anna Lois realized that

Lydia Dixon's Sunday School class, ca. 1930.

unless she could think of something she was not going to be able to have her lesson for the other children. Almost in desperation she said, "All right, children, bow your heads; we are going to pray for _____." As she said this, the culprit was underneath the table. Peeping through her fingers, as she began the prayer, she saw him crawl out from under the table, slip quietly into his chair and bow his head. He did not misbehave for the rest of the class. Obviously, she had found the solution to the problem.

In 1921 under the leadership of Georgia Reece, a Christian Endeavor Society was organized for the teenage group. Meetings were held each Sunday evening. There was always a good attendance even though the young people had to walk to the services most of the time (Griffin "History" 14).

In the 1940s, Elbert Newlin, the pastor, introduced a new activity for the young people in Christian Endeavor. It was called "journeying" and was done once a month. The leaders would select a member's home to visit for the evening service. The chosen member was not informed of the approaching visit and was surprised or horrified when the group descended for the evening meeting. They not only expected to have their meeting with the unsuspecting host or hostess but they expected to be served refreshments as well. Needless to say, this produced some very interesting and unusual treats. One person was heard to say that when the "journeying" began, she had fixed some peanut butter crackers and intended to keep them until the group finally came to her house. There is no record if the crackers were used or not.

Later the Friends Youth Fellowship replaced the Christian Endeavor program. In recent years, a variety of programs and incentives for attendance have been used. Members have been able to take part in yearly meeting activities such as camping at Quaker Lake, Junior and Young Friends Yearly Meeting, work camps to mission fields, and annual trips to the United Nations in New York City.

Daily Vacation Bible Schools have been held for many years in the summer, not only for the children of Cane Creek but for the

The Christian Endeavor Society, ca. 1940.

children of the community as well. It was the practice in the 1940s for visiting teams to come and assist with the Bible Schools. Waldo and Lutie Woody are well remembered for their work on such a team. Children were fascinated with their model of the Old Testament Tabernacle.

Cane Creek First Day School has changed greatly since it began shortly after the Civil War. For many years it was mostly for children. Then someone realized that adults could benefit from a Sunday School also. Sometime near the beginning of this century, the First Day Schools began to have some of the characteristics which are associated with Sunday Schools today. There were classes and lessons and teachers and superintendents and secretaries and collections.

The following account from Sunday School records will give the reader some idea of the changes which have occurred through the years, "C.C. S.S. held 10th month 27, 1901. School was opened by reading from the 5 chpt. of Matthew followed by prayer after the lesson entitled Joseph and His Brothers was read."

The classes were identified by a number and were listed with their attendance. There was a total of eighty-two present. The narrative continues, "After a collection of 14 cnts was taken for three girls in India. School closed with a song." Lizzie Thompson was the secretary and Mahlon Dixon was the superintendent. At the bottom of the page is the notation, "Anna Edgerton 11 cts. needy Bible School 8 cts."

Early Friends did not limit their efforts in the area of religious education just to the youth of the meeting. They were progressive in their desire to further the education of older Friends as well. The formation of meeting libraries was begun in response to that desire. North Carolina Yearly Meeting formulated a plan to establish a library in each monthly meeting in 1828. The plan was read at Cane Creek in November 1829. However, Cane Creek had been discussing plans for a library prior to that time. From the Minutes of Twelfth month 1829, one reads, "Plans to establish a library were discussed. Decision was deferred to next meeting."

Apparently the decision was to delay establishing a library because it was not until February 1830, that a library plan was adopted by the monthly meeting. At that meeting, Joshua Chamness was appointed librarian. His job description was to be in charge of the books belonging to the meeting and to make a report of the number and titles to the monthly meeting.

Later the Minutes of March 1830 record that a standing library committee of William Thompson, William Weisner, James Woody, Nathan Pickett, Joseph Hill, and Thomas Pugh was appointed. Peter Stout was appointed to survey members for books to be donated and to propose books to be purchased.

In May 1831, a committee was appointed to "secure subscriptions to augment the library project." Later in that same year, it was reported to the monthly meeting, "$110.17 $^{1}/_{2}$ total subscriptions. Of that $72 $^{1}/_{2}$ was in books, $31.95 in cash and 95 cents not likely to be collected."

Friends had learned the value of committee work well, for in 1848, a committee was appointed to "examine the library books and ascertain if they contained sentiments not in accordance with the doctrines maintained by our ancient predecessors" and report. One book, *Portable Evidence on Christianity*, was found to be unsuitable and excluded. On July 6, 1850, the committee asked to be released from their responsibility and the monthly meeting concurred with their request.

Few books from this period are still in existence. It is likely most were lost when the meeting burned in 1879. Those saved were with Friends at Rocky River or had been checked out to members. On July 1, 1843, the monthly meeting had approved Rocky River's request to house part of the library collection.

No library, as such, was in the present meetinghouse until 1961. Beulah Allen, a retired librarian, gave many hours of labor in organizing the library. Some books were purchased and others were donated. Shelves were built and placed in one of the Sunday School classrooms. The adult books were housed there. A separate children's library was kept in the assembly room in the church's basement. When the basement was remodeled in the 1960s, the children's books were packed away for safe keeping. Unfortunately, they were too safe; they have not surfaced to this day.

Today, the library is attractively furnished with a conference table and comfortable couches and chairs which create an atmosphere conducive to reading. The meeting is very fortunate to have had the services of Wilma Griffin, a retired public school librarian, to care for the collection.

Bascom Rollins, pastor 1946–1956, with a group of dedicated workers in the meeting. Left to right: Sarah Primm, Lyndon Stuart, Ruth Moon, Rollins, and Anna Lois Dixon.

EDUCATION

Fear not the skeptic's puny hand
While near the school the church will stand,
Nor for the blinded bigots' rule
While near the church shall stand a school

So wrote the Quaker poet, John Greenleaf Whittier; so wrote and spoke the Quakers themselves. Friends have always been "big" on education, to coin a phrase from modern youth. There are few records of early schools; however, journals and diaries testify to the fact that the pioneers were educated in varying degrees. Legacies often included the stipulation, ". . .for the education of my children."

Subscription schools were organized in the late 1700s. Parents paid a certain fee, a subscription, each time a child was enrolled. Monthly meeting records mention the payment of school costs for the children who were unable to pay. Surveys were taken regularly to determine the number of children without schooling.

In May 1832, according to the Minutes, Cane Creek planned to open a monthly meeting school. Part of the curriculum was daily Bible reading. Teachers were to be Quakers if at all possible. The schools were open to all children, members and non–members.

Four years later, James Smith, Ben Hinshaw, William Hinshaw, William Thompson, and Thomas Stout surveyed the schools. In accordance with the instructions given them by the monthly meeting, they gathered information on the number of minors, the state of the schools, and also the lack of Bibles. When the survey was finished in February 1835, they gave the following report. There were four schools, two of which were taught by Friends. They had counted 171 minors; forty–five of the minors were under five years of age, and 125 were over five years. They concluded their report with the information that the over five–year–old group received "school learning." Would it be facetious to suggest that the members of the committee should have availed themselves of a math class for their addition seems a bit lacking?

A similar report was made in February 1838. "There have been six schools within the past year — three taught by Friends and three by persons not in membership with us. All in a mixed state and all are supplied with the scriptures."

The Monthly Meeting Schools and the Subscription Schools evolved into neighborhood schools. Several were established in the area; among them, Hunting Branch, Fogleman's School, Langley School, West Point, Lancaster, Mudlick, Piedmont, and Fairmont (*Sylvanian* 14).

Lancaster School was started around 1838 and served the community for many years. The school stood south of the entrance to what is now the site of *The Sword of Peace* near the Charlie Stout House on Sylvan Road. The original log structure was replaced with a two–story frame building by the Good Templar Society and was used as their meeting place as well as for a school. The log building has survived the years but has an interesting travel history. When it was replaced, it was moved some 400 yards to the east and used by Ed Thomas for a barn. Several years later, it was moved again; this time, to the west, past the original site to become one of the buildings for visitors to the site of the outdoor drama, *The Sword of Peace* (Griffin Notes).

The Baltimore Association was interested in rebuilding the South and helping Friends recover from the Civil War. With their assistance, Cane Creek Monthly Meeting established the Sylvan of the Grove Academy in 1866. Prior to that time, there was a

Old Sylvan Academy, established 1866.

monthly meeting school in the meetinghouse. Allen J. Tomlinson of High Point was sent to Cane Creek to open the new school.

Joseph Moore, superintendent of schools for the Baltimore Association, assisted with the establishment of the academy. At first, he was somewhat doubtful that the effort would be successful, but when he visited the meeting, he found the members to be determined to go ahead with the project. He was quite pleased to find that he was proven wrong and the school was successful. His journal entries provide interesting information about the academy:

> 11th month, 19, 1866, went to Allen J. Tomlinson's school which opened this morning in the old meeting house, the school being justly weatherboarded and roofed. School making an orderly start with seventeen.

> 12th month, 12, 1866, visit A. J. Tomlinson's school about eighty pupils in very good order. Regard it quite an achievement to haste such good order where they had been accustomed to disorder. . .a day of rejoicing for me (*Sylvanian* 9).

Five months later, about 300 people attended a lecture where plans were made for an addition to the schoolhouse. Sylvan of the Grove Academy grew to be one of the largest in North Carolina. Each term there would be several boarding students who were required to pay tuition. If the students were unable to do this, the monthly meeting would pay for them. Religious instruction continued to be part of the curriculum with daily Bible reading. On Thursday, or Fifth day, all the students were taken to the meeting-house where they attended the midweek worship service. Students were also expected to attend the First day worship service as well. Often the teachers were quite active in the meeting.

One rather unusual event happened soon after the Civil War. The Baltimore Association not only helped establish schools but

Allen J. Tomlinson, first principal of Sylvan Academy

assisted with the curriculum as well. An Agriculture Club was added to the course of study at Sylvan about 1868. The Association agreed to donate a Jersey bull to the newly created department if in return the club members would pay the freight. In due time, the bull arrived with a freight bill of $50. The club members thought this bill was excessive and refused to pay it.

Caleb Dixon decided to pay the bill and thus he became the owner of a Jersey bull named Sherman; appropriately so, some thought. Sherman soon became the scourge of the neighborhood. He would wander over the fields tearing down the rail fences as he went and generally creating havoc. The only person who seemed able to control him was the youngest member of the Dixon family, Zeno Dixon. He was about twelve years old at this time, and Sherman would allow him to lead him about with a chain and also ride upon his back.

The bull could not be controlled, however, and eventually Mr. Dixon decided to sell him. In 1876, Zeno mounted Sherman and began a trip of about sixty miles to Raleigh where Sherman would be sold at the state fair. They got as far as Chapel Hill on the first day of the trip and created quite a stir when they rode into town. The second night was spent at Morrisville. Zeno was quite safe on the trip, because when anyone approached them, Sherman would lower his head and bellow a few times and any would–be pranksters would quickly disappear. Sherman won the first prize of $20. He was later sold to a farmer in the eastern part of the state. Thus, the Agriculture Club's first attempt at husbandry ended rather ignominiously.

Cane Creek Monthly Meeting continued to support the Sylvan Academy monetarily until 1903. At this time it was deeded to the county. In 1908 the county recognized the need to provide facilities for higher education for the students and made the former Sylvan Academy into Sylvan High School by adding one more classroom, enlarging the curriculum, and hiring one more teacher. In 1912, Isaac and Jane Allen Hammer donated 640 acres of land in Kansas as an endowment for a school in the Cane Creek community. They also gave a cash donation, to be matched by local citizens, for a new building. The matching funds were raised and construction began almost immediately (*Sylvanian* 9).

The new Sylvan School building was located south of the meetinghouse, across Cane Creek atop a small hill known as "Flint Hill" on land purchased from Cicero Dixon (*Sylvanian* 9). It was aptly named. Generations of school children could testify about innumerable skinned elbows and knees received from falls on the flint rocks.

The large two–story Georgian style building was constructed in about a year. It was during this time that the county decided to consolidate several small community schools. Thus, the building would serve a much larger population than had been originally anticipated.

School was held in the new location at the beginning of the term in 1913. The cornerstone was appropriately engraved "The Allen–Hammer Memorial. School" in appreciation for the endowment which made construction possible. Despite efforts to comply with the name change, this school would forever be known as Sylvan.

In 1960 Sylvan was consolidated with four other high schools in southern Alamance County to form Southern High School. Sylvan School is now an elementary school with grades kindergarten through fifth. A fire destroyed the original two–storied building in the 1970s. The smaller building, which survived the fire, served the school population very adequately for a number of years. However, in the 1990s, the population of Snow Camp increased when several mobile home parks were opened in the area. Consequently, the enrollment of Sylvan School ballooned making new classrooms a necessity, and a new building was begun on "Flint Hill."

Just as their forefathers did, members of Cane Creek Meeting support the school and take much interest in their children's education.

CONCERN FOR MISSIONS AND OUTREACH

To do missions without serving the needs of those whose spiritual and physical condition must change is to carry an empty, hypocritical gospel.

These words spoken so aptly in the 1980s at a session of North Carolina Yearly Meeting could have been spoken just as appropriately in the late 1700s, for they succinctly state what must have been the motivation for missions at Cane Creek Monthly Meeting during the early years. Then missions meant a concern for the well–being of others, whether it be for an individual or an entire meeting. This principle is exemplified by the following Minute: First month 1781, David

Smith was appointed by the monthly meeting to "inquire into the sufferings of Friends and to report as to their needs." One can only assume that steps were taken by the monthly meeting to meet any existing needs that were reported.

Neither was it unusual for persons to ask the monthly meeting for assistance in personal matters. In 1784, "A concern for care was expressed by William Courtney, brother of James and Joseph Courtney, both blind, asking Friends to procure maintenance for them." This was done. Similar incidents and requests were recorded throughout the next century.

Almost one hundred years later, in June 1873, Sarah Wilson had a concern to visit "some that are afflicted, and also to visit the Poor House in Randolph County." The monthly meeting united in encouraging her to attend "as wisdom dictates."

One of the more enterprising projects was the construction in the late 1800s of a two–room house, just north of the meetinghouse near the spring, for the use of an elderly woman who had no means of support. Not only did the meeting build her a house, but it also assumed the responsibility of providing food and other necessities for her. After her death, the little house, affectionately known as the "Abigail House" was used for a classroom at Sylvan School (Griffin "History" 37).

In a similar vein and more recently, the Quaker men's organization, in collaboration with Mount Pleasant Methodist Church, built a house for a black family whose home was old and dilapidated. Once, the monthly meeting even rented a woman's land so that she could have an income. It has always been the custom to provide firewood for those persons in the community who have difficulty in procuring their own.

Cane Creek's concern for the needs of the people was not confined to the surrounding areas. Ways of communication improved between communities, between monthly meetings, and between yearly meetings in direct proportion to the increase in population. Better communication alerted the monthly meeting to the needs of people not only nearby but in faraway places as well. The scene was set for a more far–reaching concern in the area of foreign missions. It was this concern which gave birth to the women's missionary movement.

A leader in the organization of the Women's Missionary Union and the first editor of its monthly magazine, *The Advocate*, was a birthright member of Cane Creek: Eliza Clark Armstrong Cox. She was the daughter of Alexander and Ann Johnson Clark, who were married September 5, 1840. The monthly meeting appointed Ruth Stafford and Lydia Pugh to attend the ceremony and entertainment. They did as instructed and later reported that they "saw nothing disorderly" (Griffin "History" 38).

Eliza Clark was born February 6, 1850. When she was six years old, her grandfather, Dougan Clark, a Friends minister, encouraged the family to move to Indiana to escape the evils of slavery. They settled at Monrovia and joined the West Union Friends Meeting. At the age of twenty–seven, Eliza Clark married Joshua Armstrong. Eight years after his death, she married Joseph Cox, also a Quaker.

It was in Indiana that the idea for a society for Friends women was born. She learned that some of the Quaker women from her local meeting were attending a women's foreign missionary society at a local Methodist Episcopal Church. She reasoned, correctly, that if the Quaker women had a desire to do this kind of service, they should have a society of their own (Hinshaw and Hockett 1).

She immediately began work to make her idea become a reality. Soon she found others with similar ideas, and, in March 1891, the first organization was formed at Hopewell Meeting in Indiana.

Within a few weeks eight local societies had been formed through-out Western Yearly Meeting. When representatives met at the sessions of Western Yearly Meeting in September of that year, a formal organization was formed and Eliza Armstrong Cox was selected as its head

Through correspondence with relatives the women of North Carolina caught the idea of a Woman's Missionary Society. In 1885, at Yearly Meeting, the Woman's Foreign Missionary Society was organized with a twofold purpose: "to spread the Gospel among the heathen, and for the elevation of women in the Yearly Meeting." In 1925 the Triennial Conference of the Women's Missionary Union met in Greensboro. Eliza Armstrong Cox was there and was described as "a tiny, lively, saintly woman" (Hinshaw and Hockett 2–6).

It was at this time that she paid a visit to her birthplace in the Cane Creek community. When she arrived she stood in the yard for a moment, looked at her surroundings, and then said, "Leave me alone and I will show you the spring and the location of the pig pen." Within minutes she had located the spring and walked to the spot where the pig pen had stood. She explained that she would never forget that spot, for one morning, as she watched her father feed the pigs, she poked a finger through the fence and a pig bit off the end of her finger (Griffin "History" 39).

The Women's Missionary Society of Cane Creek was orga-nized about 1910. Miles Reece came to Sylvan School as a teacher in 1909. His wife, Georgia Griffith Reece, had been a missionary in Jamaica. She soon generated enough interest among the women of the meeting to organize the first missionary society. From that time until the present, the women have continued to meet monthly.

During the late 1930s and 1940s there were two missionary circles. One met in the afternoon and soon became known as the

Quilters, ca. 1940. Left to right, Anna Lois Dixon, Kathlene Whitehead, Nona Williams, Christine McPherson, Mildred Durham, Verla Thompson, Phoebe Pike, Annie Wright, Lena Durham, Gertrude Pike, Inez Williams, Kathryn Carter, Alice Teague, Lorena Thompson, Ruth Moon.

"Old Women's Circle," leaving one to surmise that the night circle was for "young women." The mid–century years of the 1950s became the glory years with four night circles, one afternoon circle, a junior missionary group for young teens which met on Saturday afternoons, and also a group for older teens and unmarried young women. At the present time the count is back to two, one at night and one in the afternoon.

Some excerpts from the circle minute books indicate the interest and the work of the various groups. For example, the junior missionary group met with Mattie Thompson, their sponsor and adult advisor, in October 1945. There were six members present, 181 Bible chapters read, twenty–three visits to shut–ins and four bunches of flowers "carried." A coloring contest was discussed with twenty–five cents offered as first prize. Second prize was fifteen cents. Joanna Thompson was the secretary.

The Hackney Reece Circle, composed of older members, met in the afternoon once a month for many years. On July 19, 1944, they met at Lucy Kimball's home with twelve members present. It was recorded that their membership was twenty–nine "paid–up" members. Also, their circle had been rated a "standard society" according to the "attainments" set by the yearly meeting union. It is unclear what this entailed.

In an earlier Minute from this same circle one reads, "The best way to win a family to Christ is by first winning the mother 'because she is so ignorant'." Hopefully this statement was taken out of context by the recording secretary!

Today the work and influence of the Women's Missionary Society continues to be strong. In many areas tradition is upheld as the modern society member often makes beautiful quilts for sale at fund–raising activities, sews for the American Friends Service Committee, provides meats and vegetables for the annual Brunswick stew sale, and, as the junior circle did years ago, reads Bible chapters, sends cards, visits shut–ins, and carries flowers.

A QUAKER CUSTOM,
A QUAKER TESTIMONY

The custom of disownment was practiced extensively in the early Quaker meetings. It was considered a deterrent to misconduct and was enacted in a loving and caring environment. The root causes of many disownments could be traced to the use of alcoholic beverages. Friends developed a strong temperance testimony in an effort to overcome the detrimental effects of alcohol upon society.

The practice of disownment became more prevalent as the Society of Friends grew and spread. Every religious group has rules and regulations for its members to follow, and Friends are no exception. However, in the Quaker faith, there is no formal creed but rather a statement of faith.

Early Friends considered themselves a people "apart" from the world and, as such, did not want things or people of the world to infringe on or interfere with their way of life. They dressed plainly and condemned worldly ideas and pleasures. Marrying out of the fellowship of believers and associating with persons overly concerned with worldly matters such as politics and war were considered serious violations of the rules of discipline which had been made for their daily living as well as for their spiritual well–being.

Any indiscretion that others saw as an impediment to their faith would be duly reported to the monthly meeting in the form of a complaint. A committee of "weighty Friends" would be appointed to visit the culprit and try to convince the person of his mistake. If the person were not willing to admit his error, a second or third visit might be made. If the matter could not be settled satisfactorily, the committee would advise disownment.

On the other hand, if the individual were willing to prepare a paper condemning his or her conduct, the monthly meeting would accept it and the matter would be dropped. Should the person refuse to condemn his own actions, the monthly meeting would disown him.

A typical paper of condemnation was recorded in the 1890s:

To Cane Creek Monthly Meeting of Friends, I have been overtaken and am guilty of immoral conduct of which I am very sorry ask monthly meeting to forgive me and by the Lord's help I will endeavor to live a consistent life (Griffin Notes).

Perhaps a more enlightening paper would be in answer to the inevitable question, "What happened in a marriage that had been performed out of unity with the meeting, if one of the partners condemned his or her own actions and asked for forgiveness?"

The Minutes of Cane Creek Monthly Meeting bear mute

testimony to the large number of members who were disowned during the nineteenth century. In fact, a local wag has made the statement, "Our church [Methodist] would never have grown much if the Quakers had ever stopped disowning people."

The Minutes of the meeting record many various reasons for disownments. Some border on the trivial; some seem almost hilarious to the modern reader. It is important to realize they were neither trivial nor hilarious to the individual involved — or to the meeting.

Some of the more serious reasons for disownment were marrying out of unity, marrying contrary to discipline, going into a society of different persuasion (for example, Methodist), retailing spiritous liquors, keeping unlawful company with another man's wife, not attending meeting, departing from plain living, having carnal knowledge of his wife before marriage, holding and selling slaves, refusing to pay a note of indebtedness, having a child in an unmarried state, attending a mustering, paying a military fee, accusing women's meeting of falsifying Minutes.

Other reasons which appear to be more trivial to the reader today are tale bearing, dancing or trying to dance, wearing hair disagreeable to Friends, showing a dislike to a friend in a time of prayer, enclosing and claiming sheep belonging to a neighbor, helping a brother steal a young woman to marry, throwing rocks, and using profanity. When the last reason was given as a complaint the meeting changed the charge to "using unseemly language."

One instance of condemning one's own conduct that was not beneficial is told of a Friend who had made a name for himself as a teller of very tall tales. The usual procedures were taken after someone complained about him to the monthly meeting. In due time, the committee which had been appointed to talk with him arrived at his home and spent several hours with him pointing out the error of his ways. Finally, he was asked if he were sorry for his actions. He replied, "Oh, yes, I have already shed a barrel of tears."

The monthly meeting never acted hastily in the matter of disownments. Some times months would elapse before the matter could be settled. The Herman Husband affair, for example, took fifteen months to settle.

Disownments rarely occur any more. Originally, perhaps, there may have been merit in such action. Early Friends certainly believed that the practice was necessary; in reality it proved to be otherwise. Allen Thomas, in *A History of Friends in America*, seems to say it best, "That the denomination should have lived at all through such restrictions is a striking evidence of the power that was in the body [of believers]" (193).

The Cane Creek Meeting had a great concern about the use of spiritous liquor and the problems resulting from its use and sale. Numerous members were disowned for using spiritous liquor to excess, for retailing the same, and also for the distillation of it. In other words, they were greatly disturbed about those persons who made, sold, or used alcohol.

Committees were appointed by the monthly meeting each year to take a survey every three months to find who used intoxicating liquors and who did not. According to the Minutes of August 1844, it was reported that the results of a survey revealed 115 people who did not use alcoholic beverages and ten who did use them. The report also listed those who used alcohol for medicinal purposes.

Perhaps the low number of persons who used alcohol could, in part, be attributed to the organization of the Pleasant Hill Temperance Society in 1833. This organization's goal was to inform and ultimately wipe out the use of "spiritous liquors." William Albright, a local medical doctor, was the founder and guide for many years. Cane Creek joined the society along with several other churches in the area. Over the years attendance and membership dropped until only Cane Creek and Pleasant Hill remained as members. The meetings were held twice a year. Pleasant Hill hosted the meeting on the Fourth of July each year and Cane Creek's turn was on Christmas Day. This organization continued to function until the 1950s. On the 100th anniversary of its founding, an all–day program was held at Pleasant Hill. The speaker was Judge Johnson J. Hayes. The major concern of the meeting was the repeal of the eighteenth amendment. At the meeting, 310 new members were added to the membership. There is no record of the entire membership (Society Minutes 1933).

There were two other temperance civic organizations in the area in the 1800s: the Good Templars and the Sons of Temperance. The former was particularly influential in the area. Their sole purpose seems to have been the control of intoxicating liquors (Griffin "History" 34).

In January 1909, Cane Creek appointed a Temperance Committee composed of Eula Dixon, Flora Stout, J. Randolph Coble, and W. Taylor Pickett. Their duties were "to call the attention of the meeting to such matters relating to temperance reform both state and national, insist on vigilant support of our state prohibition laws by the entire membership, encourage scientific temperance instruction in the public schools, and give a written report to the monthly meeting at the end of the church year."

Quakers did not always take part in civil affairs, but in the matter of temperance they were quite active. In 1933, the monthly meeting enlisted the aid of State Representative Gilliam in getting the North Carolina Legislature to pass a bill prohibiting the sale of beer within one and one–half miles of the meeting and school. The bill was passed. A few years ago, however, it could not be enforced.

CANE CREEK COMMUNITY

T he Cane Creek community has not been conducive to commercial enterprise through the years. Attempts have been made to establish some kind of industry in the community from time to time, but none of them has been successful enough to withstand the test of time. It is almost as if fate has decided that Snow Camp should forever remain a small village in a pastoral setting.

In the beginning each pioneer family was fairly self–sufficient. They learned to "make do with what they had or do without." For the first fifty years the people of Snow Camp were primarily interested in survival. All of their efforts were expended toward the establishment of their homes, farms, and their meeting. They were busy sending roots deep into the Carolina soil.

There were times when the pioneers found it expedient to share the skills of one another. One of the earliest traditions among them was that of banding together to "raise a cabin or a barn." When a need arose, there was no hesitancy on the part of the frontier men or women to share their skills or provide a service. For example, Rachel Allen was a "doctor." She had a knowledge of various herbs, wild plants, and homemade remedies which she would prescribe for pioneer aches and pains. It is said that she kept her "medicine" in the little room at the rear of their cabin. People came to her for help or she would make "housecalls" (*Alamance Battleground*). There is no indication that she charged for her assistance; perhaps grateful patients would have given her some token of appreciation. By a very large stretch of the imagination, one might say this was Snow Camp's first pharmacy.

The tendency to work together and share their corporate skills grew in direct proportion to the increasing number of people coming into the Snow Camp area. The first businesses were probably begun when one skill was traded for another. For instance, a man with the tools and skill of a blacksmith might shoe a horse for his neighbor. In return, the neighbor might repair the smithy's harnesses. This kind of exchange could have been parlayed into a small business by an enterprising pioneer.

Some settlers came to the community with the intention of establishing a business, perhaps as a sideline for the primary purpose of farming. They carried with them any tools they would need for this secondary purpose. Simon Dixon with his millstones is a good example. Others came equally prepared for similar endeavors.

The first industry in the Snow Camp area was grist mills. The economic premise of supply and demand made this an attractive business opportunity which continued into the twentieth century. An interview with Wilma Griffin provided the information about the first industries and stores in the Snow Camp community.

South of Snow Camp approximately two and one–half miles on state road 1004, commonly known as the Snow Camp Road, one can turn right onto the Old Dam Road. The road built over the old dam is all that remains of a grist mill built by Jones Cantor around 1875. The small dam provided enough power for a saw mill as well as the grist mill. The mill had various owners, some for only a short time: Franklin Hinshaw, Tyree Hinshaw, Maurice Stuart, and, the last one, Wesley Routh. This mill became inoperable about 1930.

In 1885 the Little Ward Mill was built about two miles west of the Cane Creek Meetinghouse on a tributary of Cane Creek. This mill building stands on the property of Juanita Euliss.

Apparently, then as now, diversification became necessary for businesses to succeed. South of Sylvan School on Chamness' Creek, William Thompson not only ground wheat but also made rifles and chairs, ginned cotton, and ran a wool carding operation as well. Two generations after Simon Dixon's death, the Dixon family found it necessary to expand their operation by ginning cotton and doing some foundry work. Murphy Williams in the 1930s and 1940s would also use part of the Dixon mill for a cabinet shop. Examples of his craft can still be found in the community.

At one time there were two foundries in operation in Snow Camp. The Snow Camp Foundry stood on the north bank of the Cane Creek about two miles downstream from Dixon's mill. Since water power was the energy source of that time for mills and factories, a dam was usually built before the factory itself. Jesse Dixon, with a team of oxen, built the dam across Cane Creek to supply power for his new business. He called his new venture the Snow Camp Manufacturing Company, but it would forever be called "the foundry" by local people.

Snow Camp's second foundry was built by Timple Unthank around the year 1850. It was known as the Fairmount Foundry. After the Civil. War, it was reorganized and expanded by D. H. Albright, W. J. Stockard, Nathan Stafford, and William Henley. It stood about two miles south of the Snow Camp Foundry on what is today Workman Road. Business boomed for both foundries after the Civil War. Jobs in the foundries were much sought after. A few cabins were provided for the workers but most of the employees lived in their own homes in the area. Competition for the sale of foundry products increased with the establishment of foundries in nearby towns. The cost of production also mounted, and eventually neither of the foundries found it feasible to continue operation. By 1900, both had ceased production.

Snow Camp did not escape the insurgence of the textile

industry into Alamance County. At about the same time that E. M. Holt was beginning his textile empire some ten miles northwest of Snow Camp on the Little Alamance Creek, the Snow Camp Cotton Factory began operation in 1835. The company was composed of one thousand stockholders. In just a few years, they had bought four acres of land from Peter Stout, made bricks by the thousands, and constructed a three–story brick building to house their new endeavor. This building stood about a mile downstream from the Snow Camp Foundry.

At that point on the river, Peter Stout had previously built a small dam. This dam was very unusual, for it curved across the river rather than being straight. He built it to furnish power for his saw mill. It was not high enough to provide the force needed to run cotton mill machinery so the dam had to be raised several feet. The large stones were quarried about one–half mile upstream and floated down to the dam site.

Snow Camp Highway Marker

Workers were housed in small log cabins behind the mill. This may have been the first mill village in Alamance County. A number of wells and at least one remaining house bear testimony to the village's location.

In 1885 the factory was sold to a Mr. Willard from Massachusetts. Later he willed the mill and property to two Holman brothers, and it has remained in their family through the years. The mill stood idle for a few years but reopened in 1893 and continued with various types of manufacturing until 1937. The big metal waterwheel was sold for scrap metal during World War II.

About one mile west of the cotton factory, also on the banks of Cane Creek, was another textile industry, the Snow Camp Woolen Mill. It was located on the site of the Snow Camp Foundry. It was started in 1886 by Hugh and Thomas C. Dixon. The woolen mill produced blankets, flannel material, and knitting yarn. It employed a dozen people who were paid about $1.00 a day. Meager by comparison with the wages of the present time, it was a very good salary then. Similar jobs in other textile factories in Burlington paid only about $.50 a day. The Dixons tried to provide good working conditions for their employees. Two small houses were built to accommodate those workers who did not live within walking distance of the mill.

The tin covered building would have been very hot in summer and cold in winter. There were tall windows across the front and sides for light and ventilation. Much care had to be taken with the heating arrangements in the winter because of the volatile nature of the materials used.

The two Dixons hoped to leave a stable and well–established business to their heirs. This was not to be the case for Hugh's son, Joe, had other ideas. He did not want to run the mill, preferring to go West and seek his fortune there. Joe prevailed on a friend of his to come into the family business in his place. This incident set the stage for Tom McVey to assume a prominent role in the life of the community.

Tom McVey was born in the Snow Camp community in 1859. He was educated at Sylvan Academy and New Garden Boarding School (later Guilford College). He was a firm supporter of education for all persons. After his graduation he became a teacher in Moore County, where he met and married Fanny Tyson. When he became a rather reluctant half–owner of the Snow Camp Woolen Mill in 1893, the direction of his life changed, but he never lost his dedication to education (Hughes).

Despite his reluctance, Tom McVey proved to be a good business man and undoubtedly was proud of his business acuity. He was also keenly interested in politics and was an ardent Republican. He served the constituency of Snow Camp for three terms as county commissioner. One of the highlights of his life was meeting President Taft in Washington. This meeting could well have been arranged by his friend, Joe Dixon, who had been very successful in Montana. Dixon was governor of that state and later was appointed United States Assistant Secretary of the Interior.

Tom McVey was secretary and treasurer of the woolen mill. The president was also an unusual person who would play an important role in the Snow Camp community. Her name was Eula Dixon. While Tom may have come to the mill by default, Eula inherited her share from her father, Thomas Dixon.

Eula Dixon was born during the period of reconstruction of the South following the Civil. War. She was a great granddaughter of Simon Dixon and exhibited the same kind of dedication, determi-nation, and tenacity to do a task well, as Simon had exhibited as he helped to settle a new home and community (Hobbs).

Eula Dixon was a pioneer in women's rights, although it is

Eula Dixon

doubtful that she would have described herself in those terms. Born in a time in history when a woman's place was considered by the vast majority of people to be in the home, she was indeed an exception to that train of thought. When her father died in 1899, she assumed the responsibility for the family farm as well as presidency of the woolen mill. When she was thirty years old, she became the first woman student to attend the State Agriculture and Mechanical Arts College in Raleigh. When she returned home, she put into practice the knowledge she had acquired. Her plantation became one of the best in the area. Together, she and Tom McVey made many improvements at the woolen mill and greatly increased its productivity.

Tom McVey and Eula Dixon were alike in many ways. They both had a great love for Cane Creek Meeting assuming active roles in various capacities. They were both keenly interested in good education for all persons, and both served terms as the chairperson of the local school board.

Eula relinquished her role in the woolen mill soon after Tom died in 1910. The mill burned in 1912. The owners were reluctant to invest in repairs. Thus, the textile industry came to an end in Snow Camp.

A contributing factor to the failure of the factories and the foundries was a lack of good transportation. The raw material for both had to be brought by wagon over many miles of sometimes almost impassable roads. The market for their products was many miles away. As the productivity of both factories and farms increased, the problem of poor roads became greater. It became necessary for the farmer and the factory owner to seek a solution to the problem.

The idea of a plank road was born. A road made of planks would provide a stable surface over which wagons loaded with produce and supplies could travel easily. A company known as the Graham Gulf Plank Road Company was formed. John Stafford was the president and H. W. Dixon was vice president. Construction began in 1853 (Griffin Notes).

The road was to have begun in Graham, go southward to Gulf where it would intersect with the Salem plank road and continue on to Fayetteville. For some unknown reason, the road began in Snow Camp rather than Graham. Perhaps it was because Hugh Dixon set up a saw mill to cut the planks near Snow Camp.

There were toll stations every seven miles. The one at Snow Camp stood on the north side of Cane Creek just before the road crossed the bridge. A teamster would purchase tickets for his trip at the first toll station he came to. He would have paid between two and one–half cents to five cents a mile, depending on the number of horses he had and how heavily his wagon was loaded. The teamster's destination was noted on each ticket. He was expected to turn in all the tickets when he arrived at his destination and failure to do so resulted in a fine. Each toll station bore a reminder, "Pay toll, give up tickets or pay fine." A generally understood rule for drivers on the plank road was that if going downhill, the driver could use all the plank. Other times, he could only use half.

After the Civil War there was no money for maintenance of the road, so it fell into disrepair and eventual disuse. Gradually, it rotted away or was covered with dirt. Even in recent years, portions of the plank road have been found as new excavations have been made for modern roads.

When the initial grading for the Snow Camp–Siler City road was done, not only parts of the plank road were found but a human skeleton as well. It was not identifiable but some older residents thought it might have solved a mystery of many years. A Mr. Vincent had disappeared without a trace several years before. Foul play was suspected, but no body was ever found. The skeleton could be that of Mr. Vincent. How clever his murderer to stuff the body under the planks of the road! The only question still unanswered is the identification of the murderer.

Snow Camp residents continued to try to improve their transportation problem. In 1828 an effort was made to bring a line of the railroad near or through Snow Camp. Two hundred people met at the home of William Albright to discuss the matter. The railroad was strange and unknown to many of them. The meeting did not achieve the desired results, as the railroad was built several miles to the north of Snow Camp. There is a story that has been told for many years concerning one of the attenders at the meeting. This particular man rose to voice his opposition to the railroad coming to Snow Camp. He posed this question: "We will be safe as long as the train comes through as it is supposed to — longways — but what will we do if it ever comes through sideways?"

Another type of industry did rather well in Snow Camp for a number of years. Tom and Tim Boggs ran a successful pottery shop on property which is owned today by Bill Roach of Liberty. Most of the pottery was made for utilitarian purposes such as crocks for milk or cream. There were also small mouthed jugs which could hold cider, vinegar, or any other "liquid" which might be made locally. Their wares were taken into nearby cities for sale. Today their products demand a substantial price if a piece can be found for sale.

The mercantile business has been only slightly more successful than industry in Snow Camp. Through the years there have been several stores in and around the village. There was a company store operated by the cotton factory. It became Holman's Store when the ownership of the factory changed. As was the policy of most company stores, the workers could charge their purchases and the amount would be deducted from their paychecks . The first store stood northeast of the mill near the river. Later it was moved to the other side of the mill where it was more accessible to other customers. The store remained in business for many years after the cotton factory closed and was a favorite gathering place in the community. A trip to the store was enjoyed not only to buy but to socialize as well. The storekeepers were exceedingly careful in keeping the accounts. The store ledgers often reveal much more than the cost of the purchases. One such storekeeper recorded the sale of a bottle of whiskey for the mother of the purchaser. He carefully noted that it was her medicine.

The Snow Camp Market is located on the site of at least two earlier stores. Hayes Thompson had a small general store there long before there was an intersection. When Mr. Thompson moved sometime in the late 1920s, Ed Griffin and Everett Durham built a new store building at that location. It was considered quite modern for its time. It had a wide portico which extended out over the gasoline pumps. The pumps had glass bulbs at the top which held several gallons of gasoline. A manually operated lever pumped the gasoline up into the bulb. The force of gravity caused the gasoline to flow downward through a hose into the gas tank of a car. There was a large two–story feed building adjacent to the store with apartments on the second floor. When the Chapel Hill Road was built, the store building was too close to the intersection for safety. It was torn down and the present building replaced it.

South of the Snow Camp Market at the foot of the hill is the site of the old post office building. For many years the post office occupied the left corner of the building. The rest of the space was a general store operated by the Cobles. It was also the site of community gatherings from time to time. In the 1940s it was a makeshift health clinic. The county health department held mass inoculations for typhoid, diphtheria, and whooping cough. People from miles around would gather at the post office on the day appointed for "shots." They came early for it was a great time of visiting with friends. Finally, the nurses would arrive, set up their equipment under a big tree and begin. The children found it fun to watch and see who among their cohorts would cry and who would not.

Henry Hornaday operated a store at the corner of the Snow Camp and Sylvan School roads. It was close by the route many children took as they walked to school just up the hill. Sometimes mothers would send eggs to the store by their children in the morning to trade for some staple which the children would stop for at the store on their way home.

After Mr. Hornaday sold the store and moved away, the

SNOW CAMP COMMUNITY
1994

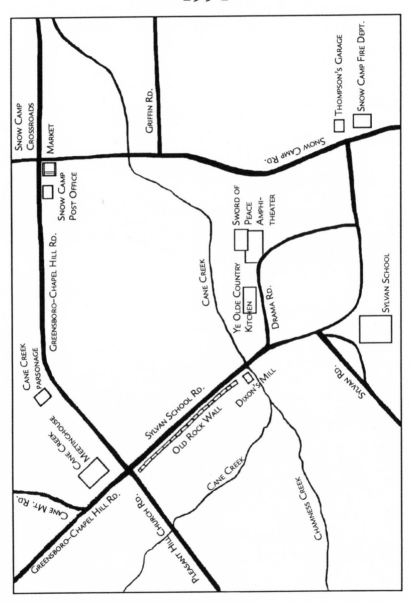

building changed ownership several times. Finally, Hayes Thompson decided to continue his career as a merchant and he bought it. It probably was at that time that the building was moved across the road to its present location. Hayes's son, F. Paul Thompson, and his wife ran the store for a number of years. The store building remains, but it has been converted to an apartment building.

Bill Fogleman ran Snow Camp's smallest store. It was in front of his house on the road that led from Griffin's store to the Cane Creek Meetinghouse. It was only about twelve feet by fifteen feet with a small roof extension at the front. Mr. Fogleman stocked a few staples primarily as a service to his neighbors. He ran a much larger store near Little Ward Mill. Since this was some miles away, it was much more convenient for some of his customers to come to the little store. However, it was not more convenient for Mr. Fogleman, for he traveled between the stores each day.

Today, Snow Camp is a quiet little village. There is no industry. There is one grocery store, two garages, a restaurant, and a post office. There are still several farms in the area, but, for the most part, people commute to nearby towns to work. It is only a sleepy little village not too far removed from its beginnings.

THE SWORD OF PEACE

The Snow Camp Historical Drama Society and ultimately *The Sword of Peace,* an outdoor drama, grew out of a chance remark made by a visitor in the home of Ed and Lorraine Griffin in the late 1960s. The visitor was a young man, Bobby Wilson, from Morganton, North Carolina, who had recently moved to the area. He was enthralled by the Griffins' stories about the settlement of the Snow Camp area. His interest prompted him to exclaim, "This is good enough for an outdoor drama." And so it was.

The idea grew and spread. People began to consider seriously the possibility of a drama, which for many would be the story of their ancestors. Bobby's brother, James Wilson, joined the effort and promoted it at every opportunity in his local cafe. Soon the Snow Camp Historical Drama Society was formed on January 20, 1971. A ground swell of community support was generated at a meeting for "all interested persons" at the Cane Creek Meetinghouse in the spring of that year. The overflow crowd of more than 400 persons emphasized the fact that this was a project in which a good number of people were very interested. It soon proved to be more than a community project, for it quickly caught the interest of people in the surrounding areas and in the five counties adjacent to Alamance.

A drama for Snow Camp was soon the topic of conversation in many places. It seemed that everyone had an idea of what should be done and how to accomplish it, and they were willing to tell anyone who would listen. Such was the case one afternoon for three of the more enthusiastic supporters. They were driving along so engrossed in the discussion of future plans that they did not notice the car was gradually slowing down and wobbling quite decidedly. Their discussion was soon halted by a blue light and a siren. They quickly pulled over to the side of the road. It was rather difficult to make the patrolman understand that all they were doing was talking. Eventually he did believe them and let them continue on their way with the parting admonition, "Hold it in the road."

Confidently armed with the community support, Wilma Griffin, Bobby Wilson, and Clara Winslow met with Mark Sumner of the Institute of Outdoor Drama at Chapel Hill. His suggestions proved invaluable to the fledgling society.

Members of the Snow Camp Historical Drama Society began immediately to bring their dream to reality. A slide presentation was created to capture the interest of possible supporters, volunteers, civic organizations, nearby churches, and local businesses. A portion of land south of the Cane Creek just off the Sylvan School Road was leased from Algie Stephens and Joe Coble for a nominal fee. William Hardy was chosen to write the script. A formal ground–breaking ceremony with Governor Robert Scott was held and the society met their first year's funding goal of $21,000.

Ironically, the initial grading for the amphitheater which would be used for a drama dealing with peace was done by a volunteer group of soldiers from Fort Bragg. They removed trees from the natural slope of land along the banks of Cane Creek. Jim Euliss volunteered his time and the use of his equipment to build the first access road into the site. The entire seating area was graded by Coy McPherson and his trusty bulldozer. Other volunteers helped with the utilitarian projects such as bathrooms, walkways, and parking facilities. However, the aesthetics were not neglected: the site was tastefully landscaped with flowers, shrubs, and native trees.

The Snow Camp Historical Drama Society has enjoyed continued support from the community throughout its more than twenty years of existence. Today, a number of volunteers and patrons form a nucleus from which the drama society draws its support. The volunteers traditionally man the various buildings that are open to the public prior to each evening performance. A "meet the cast" picnic is held each year to strengthen the ties between the cast and the community.

The Sword of Peace opened July 4, 1974, with a cast of twenty. The cast doubled the next year, and by 1977 a repertory schedule was begun. There was a special celebration on Sunday, July 4, 1976, to mark the 200th birthday of the United States. The celebration began with a special televised Sunday morning service program. Originally planned for the amphitheater, the program was moved to the nearby Cane Creek Meetinghouse when the weather proved to be unpleasant. Seth Hinshaw, then executive secretary of North Carolina Yearly Meeting, was the speaker for the occasion. He chose the topic "One Nation Under God."

The drama, *The Sword of Peace*, tells the story of Simon Dixon, the miller, and his wife, Elizabeth. Their quiet Quaker lives are disrupted by the events leading to the Battle of Alamance, a confrontation between the Regulators and the militia of Governor Tryon. Simon is the father figure for Thomas Hadley, a young Quaker lad who grows to young manhood as he resolves the conflict of joining others to fight for their country or remaining out of the conflict as his Quaker faith dictates. The drama culminates with Lord Cornwallis bringing his troops to Snow Camp following the Battle of Guilford Court House.

The Sword of Peace continues to enthrall audiences in a setting which, appropriately, lies a few paces east of the site of Dixon's Mill. The years have brought changes to the drama site with the addition of several buildings. Visitors can enjoy touring two early Quaker meetinghouses. The New Hope Meetinghouse was moved to the drama grounds from Randolph County near Sophia and is typical of a Quaker meeting of the 1800s. The Chatham Meetinghouse was moved from the Eli Whitney area and dates from the early part of the twentieth century. In addition there are log buildings, replicas of other buildings which would have been found in a typical small village of that era.

One of the goals of the Snow Camp Historical Drama Society was to preserve the memory of pioneers of the Cane Creek valley. With *The Sword of Peace,* it has succeeded,

Beginning in the summer of 1994, another drama, *Pathway to Freedom*, has been presented three nights each week. This is the story of the Quakers who participated in the Underground Railroad, a true pathway to freedom for many slaves in the South as they tried to escape from their owners. The work of the Quakers throughout North Carolina and other states to the north is emphasized.

With these two outdoor dramas about Quakers, the Snow Camp Historical Drama Society has been able to educate the people who come to the amphitheater about two of the important Quaker beliefs, the evils of war and the equality of all people.

INTO THE FUTURE

Today, Cane Creek Meetinghouse gazes serenely past the intersection of the Chapel Hill and Sylvan School Roads, past the fields that Simon Dixon tilled, down past the old stone wall, southward to the small stream from which it gets its name.

Time has weathered the gravestones. Red brick has replaced logs as a building material. Comfortable pews take the place of axe–scarred benches. Modern cars park where horses with wagons were once hitched.

Fortunately, some things have not changed. Men and women still gather on First day for worship. Children are loved and cared for as they are guided toward worthwhile adulthood. Older Friends are appreciated and valued. There are active concerns for the welfare for not only those persons within the Snow Camp community but within the universal community as well.

While it is true many changes have occurred through the years and what appeared to be insurmountable tragedies have disappeared with the passage of time, one thing has remained constant: the Quaker spirit lives and reaches out to the community from the meetinghouse on the hill.

APPENDICES

PASTORAL MINISTERS

1929–32 .... Cora Lee Norman

1932–36 .... Lewis and Pearl McFarland

1936–37 .... York and Alice Teague

1937–41 .... Benjamin and Pearl Millikan

1941–45 .... Elbert and Inez Newlin

1945–49 .... J. Waldo and Lutie Woody

1949–56 .... Bascom and Dovie Rollins

1956–59 .... Willie and Agnes Frye

1959–62 .... Robert and Lola Crow

1962–65 .... Kenneth and Hope Wood

1965–67 .... John and Sarah Kennerly

1967–68 .... Bob and Pam Medford

1968–72 .... Mark and Olivia Hodgin

1972–76 .... Hadley and Anne Robertson

1976–83 .... John and Sharon Sides

1983–87 .... Don and Virginia Osborne

1987–89 .... Don and Ann Tickle

1989– .... Dale and Marilyn Matthews

STATISTICAL REPORT 1881

Number of meetings for worship .... 2, First and Fifth days

Members 350

    Men 159

    Female 191

Additions

    By request 16

    Certificate 0

    Birth .... <u>7</u>

    Total 23

Subtractions

    Disownments 0

    By certificate 5

    Resignation 0

    Death .... <u>4</u>

    Total 9

Gain

    Under 6 50

    Children 6–21 79

Families

    Whole 52

    Parts 61

Average age at death

    Years 35

    Month

    Days

Number recorded

    ministers 2

Meetings with no

    ministers 0

Use of Scriptures

    Daily 27

    Occasionally 70

    Neglect 8

Tobacco:

    No. who use it 113

    No. who cultivate 21

    No. who sell it 5

Spirits

    Number using spirits

    as a drink 4

STATISTICAL REPORT 1981

Number of members last year 231
Additions 14
Losses 9
No. members now 236
No. households 85
Meeting for worship 118
Sunday School 84
FYF —
Monthly Meeting.. 15
Sunday evening... 0

Members contributions $25,000.00
Special donations 1,500.00
Investment or interest income 880.94
Fund raising projects.. 6,955.65
All other... 9,700.55
    Total Funds $44,037.14

To employed personnel.. $16,652.20
Christian education program 1,361.68
Maintenance 7,476.27
Capital expenditures 7,178.73
Investments made 00.00
Paid on indebtedness 2,700.00
All other.. 200.00
    Total expenditures $18,764.85

Yearly meeting budget .... $ 5,472.00
Missions fund 200.00
Aged ministers fund 27.00
Quaker Lake 45.00
Church extension 1,765.61
Friends Home 50.00
All other 282.00
Friends related 150.00
Non–Friends 442.50
    Total outreach $8,434.11

    Total Disbursements $44,003.19
        (Griffin "History" 42–43)

Meeting for Sufferings

In the early days of the Society of Friends in England, persecution was severe. A Meeting for Sufferings was instituted to assist members who were undergoing hardship and acute suffering. In the course of time, after persecutions had ceased, the name of this group was retained for a long time. In Carolina its function was to act for the yearly meeting when it was not in session. Later the Meeting for Sufferings became the Permanent Board. Now it is called Representative Body.

The Charleston Fund

The Quaker meeting in Charleston, South Carolina, was laid down in 1837. The property that was left, a house and lot, provided an annual income to the Philadelphia Yearly Meeting who held the title. In 1875, the income was $12,000. Of that, $4,000 was reserved to build a meetinghouse in Charleston whenever there would be sufficient interest. In 1876, the South Carolina Legislature authorized Friends to spend part or all of the $4,000 in building or in repairing meetinghouses elsewhere. Several North Carolina meetings were helped by this fund (Weeks 394).

The Baltimore Association of Friends

Northern and Southern Friends were not divided or separated by the Civil War, as were most other religious denominations. All American yearly meetings and others, including London and Dublin, formed an organization through which their sympathy for the suffering of Southern Friends could be expressed. This was called "The Baltimore Association to Advise and Assist Friends in Southern States."

Under the leadership of Francis T. King, a wealthy Quaker businessman of Baltimore, this organization rendered enormous assistance to Southern Friends. The sum of $138,300 was raised and spent, mostly in North Carolina, truly a great achievement for that day. The first assistance to arrive was food and clothing. After immediate needs were met, attention was turned to the rebuilding of meetinghouses. Then came the reestablishment of schools and the building of schoolhouses.

As leader, Francis T. King made two trips to England and forty trips to North Carolina. Many other workers came, such as Joseph Moore and Allen Jay. These men recognized the importance of getting children back into school, many of whom had already lost four or five years. A pattern was set for the reestablishment of the public school system in the South. In brief it might be said that, in a time when the continued existence of North Carolina Yearly Meeting was uncertain, the assistance of the Baltimore Association enabled Southern Quakerism to survive. Its work was discontinued in 1891.

WORKS CITED

Alamance Battleground Colonial Living Materials for Classrooms. Alamance, NC: Alamance Battleground Historical Society, 1991.

Coble, Finley. Personal Interview. January 29, 1993.

Cook, Albert. *Immigration of the Irish Quakers into Pennsylvania 1682–1750 With Early History in Ireland.* Baltimore: Genealogical Society, 1969.

Crow, Robert. "History of Cane Creek Meeting." Unpublished Manuscript, 1962. Cane Creek Meeting Library.

Dixon, Eula. "One of State's Historical Spots." Unpublished Manuscript, n.d. Cane Creek Meeting Library.

Faith and Practice. Book of Discipline. North Carolina Yearly Meeting of Friends, 1985.

Forbish, Bliss. *A History of Baltimore Yearly Meeting of Friends.* Sandy Springs, MD: Baltimore Yearly Meeting, 1972.

Griffin, Wilma. "History of Cane Creek Meeting." Unpublished Manuscript, 1989. Cane Creek Meeting Library.

_____. Personal Notes, n.d. Cane Creek Meeting Library.

Haines, Lee. *Micajah McPherson, A Layman with Convictions.* Marion: Wesleyan Church Heritage Brochure #3, 1977.

Hinshaw, Mary Edith. *Pioneers in Quaker Education.* Greensboro: North Carolina Friends Historical Society, 1992.

Hinshaw, Mary Edith, and Ruth Hockett, eds. *Growth Unlimited: The Story of the United Society of Friends Women.* Centennial Edition, 1881–1981.

Hinshaw, Seth B. *The Carolina Quaker Experience.* Greensboro: North Carolina Friends Historical Society, 1984.

_____. *Friends at Holly Spring.* Greensboro: North Carolina Friends Historical Society, 1982.

Hobbs, Mary Mendenhall. "Eula Dixon." *Friends Messenger*, Vol. XXVIII, November, 1921.

Hughes, Julian. "In Days Gone By." *Burlington Times News*, 1950.

Newlin, Algie I. *Friends "At the Spring."* Greensboro: North Carolina Friends Historical Society, 1984.

Nicholson, Roy. "Freedom's Hill." Marion: Wesleyan Methodist Church, 1976.

Powell, William. *The War of the Regulation and The Battle of Alamance,* May 16, 1771. Raleigh: State Department of Archives and History, 1965.

Regulator Papers, Colonial Records Vol. VII. Raleigh: North Carolina Department of Archives and History.

Smith, Warren. *One Explorer's Glossary of Quaker Terms.* Philadelphia: Friends General Conference, 1985.

Stuart, Lyndon. "A History of Cane Creek Meeting." Unpublished Manuscript, 1955. Cane Creek Meeting Library.

Sylvanian — One Hundred Fourteen Years to Remember. Burlington, NC: Allen Hammer Endowment, 1980.

Thomas, Allen. *A History of Friends in America.* Philadelphia: Winston, 1980.

Weeks, Stephen B. *Southern Quakers and Slavery.* Baltimore: Johns Hopkins Press, 1896.

What Do Friends Believe? Planning and Promotional Council: North Carolina Yearly Meeting, 1966.

Whitaker, Walter. *Centennial History of Alamance County 1849 – 1949.* Charlotte: Dowd, 1949.

Woolman, John. *Journal.* London: J. Phillips, 1775. (Everyman's Library, London: J. M. Dent and Sons, 1922.)

Minutes

Cane Creek Monthly Meeting Minutes, 1751–1909.

Cane Creek Pastoral Committee Minutes, 1940–1948.

Cane Creek Sunday School Records, 1901.

Cane Creek Hackney–Reece Missionary Society Minutes, 1940–1950.

Cane Creek Junior Missionary Society Minutes, 1940–1950.

Pleasant Hill Temperance Society Minutes, 1930–1953.

Index